BEAUTY BEYOND
THE THRESHOLD

BEAUTY BEYOND THE THRESHOLD

HOW INTERNATIONAL VOLUNTEERING SAVED MY LIFE

TIFFANY MOSHER

NEW DEGREE PRESS

COPYRIGHT © 2020 TIFFANY MOSHER

BEAUTY BEYOND THE THRESHOLD

How International Volunteering Saved My Life

ISBN

978-1-63676-637-9 *Paperback*

978-1-63676-214-2 *Kindle Ebook*

978-1-63676-208-1 *Digital Ebook*

*To my children, may you never be afraid to explore
what lies outside of your comfort zone.*

*To the sad, the anxious, the scared, the depressed,
and the emotionally lost, this book is for you.*

CONTENTS

―――――

PROLOGUE   11

PART 1   **ROCK BOTTOM**   **15**
CHAPTER 1   THE HAUNTING REALITY   17
CHAPTER 2   ABANDONED   23
CHAPTER 3   HALF EMPTY, HALF FULL   29
CHAPTER 4   THE DEVIL'S DOORSTEP   37
CHAPTER 5   HOPE SPRINGS ETERNAL   49

PART 2   **A NEW DIRECTION**   **61**
CHAPTER 6   CROSSING THE THRESHOLD   63
CHAPTER 7   ¡PUERTO RICO SE LEVANTA!   77
CHAPTER 8   AN ACTOR AND A DIRECTOR   89
CHAPTER 9   A SELFLESS SIGNATURE   103
CHAPTER 10   PANIC! AT THE AIRPORT   111
CHAPTER 11   FOSTERING HOPE   127

PART 3	**SHE'S BACK!**	**139**
CHAPTER 12	THE HEAD VS. THE HEART	141
CHAPTER 13	ADRENALINE: A BLESSING AND A CURSE	145
CHAPTER 14	NAMASTE, KATHMANDU!	153
CHAPTER 15	AN UNPREDICTABLE JOURNEY TO MARIN	159
CHAPTER 16	BACKFILL, BUCKETS, AND BRICKS, OH MY!	175
CHAPTER 17	A NIGHT AT THE MASON'S HOUSE	187
CHAPTER 18	THERAPY ON A NEPALESE MOUNTAIN	199
CHAPTER 19	A LIFE WORTH LIVING	211
	AFTERWORD	221
	ACKNOWLEDGEMENTS	223
	APPENDIX	229

"The best way to find yourself is to lose yourself in the service of others."

—MAHATMA GANDHI

PROLOGUE

———

This isn't just any ordinary travel adventure.

I'm about to take you on a different type of journey.

As a woman who battled with depression, anxiety, and pain, I longed for renewal. More than anything, I wanted to find hope, strength, and positivity again.

How did I learn how to love myself again? Well, before I tell you, we have to turn back the clock.

In 2014, I hit rock bottom.

The years between 2006 and leading up to 2014 included some wonderful times like a new marriage, another beautiful baby, and a long-awaited graduation from college. Those years also included a painful divorce, extreme paranoia, soul-crushing anxiety, deep depression, and horrible coping skills.

I convinced myself that the only way out of the pain was to take my own life.

Did you know that there are more than 264 million people worldwide who suffer from depression?[1] I honestly had no idea that so many people battled it. I always felt that I was alone in my struggles.

———

1   "Depression," World Health Organization, accessed August 3, 2020.

To deal with my depression and anxiety, I tried various methods to cope. I tried the "wait and see" approach and thought that maybe in time everything would eventually get better on its own. I tried counseling. I was also prescribed multiple cocktails of anti-depressants and anti-anxiety medications.

However, none of those methods seemed to bring any relief. After a failed suicide attempt, I knew I had to find a better way—it was literally a life or death decision.

I needed to do something different in order to find myself again.

Author Shannon L. Alder once said, "life always begins with one step outside of your comfort zone."[2]

In my case, it was buying a plane ticket to Puerto Rico. I went to volunteer with Hurricane Maria disaster response.

As an introvert, the thought of going there alone was downright terrifying. I knew I had to let go of that fear if I wanted to fulfill my desire of helping the people in Barranquitas, Puerto Rico.

For the first time, I embraced trying something new instead of running away. I allowed myself to feel that adrenaline rush and turned it into motivation.

I would have never guessed how much completing a concrete roof repair for a gentleman named Israel would change my life for the better. As he held my hand and thanked me with tears in his eyes, Israel expressed a level of gratitude that I will never forget.

I finally felt like my life had meaning and purpose again. It was an incredible feeling to take my heartache and pain and turn them into something positive.

---

2   "Shannon L. Alder Quotes- Quotable Quote," Goodreads, accessed June 9, 2020.

I couldn't stop there! I had to find more ways to help.

What do the mountains of Puerto Rico, an indigenous Mayan village in Mexico, a small coastal town in eastern North Carolina, the cities of Chesapeake and Virginia Beach, Virginia, and a remote village in Nepal all have in common?

Those are the beautiful places I traveled solo to for the purpose of volunteering (and finding myself again, strengthening my soul, and putting the pieces of my life back together). And let me tell you, the projects I worked on were pretty amazing!

So, pack your bag, my friend! Let's take that first step, leave our comfort zones behind, and go on an awe-inspiring journey of self-discovery.

Together, we are going to discover the beauty beyond the threshold.

**Some names have been changed to protect my family's privacy.

PART ONE

ROCK BOTTOM

CHAPTER ONE

THE HAUNTING REALITY

———

"C'mon, all I need is for you to catch a tiny flame. Please?"

I had never been one to be successful at starting a campfire, and that time was no exception, especially since I was alone. The cold breeze picked up which did not help my ill attempt at creating a flame. I rearranged the four logs that I had, added a little more kindling, wadded up three paper towels, and shoved them throughout the wood. I held a lighter up to the paper towels and lit them from all different directions in my final attempt at starting a fire.

If this doesn't work, then I give up and I'm going back inside. It's so freaking cold out here!

Finally, a flame ignited, and the wood eventually started to catch more flames.

"Yay!" I squealed out loud, clapping my hands as I did a little celebration dance. I felt quite proud of myself for this small (but major for me) victory.

As quickly as the flame ignited, it calmed down. The roaring and blazing fire I had envisioned was just not going to happen, but at least there was a small fire trying with all its might to stay alive. The way the flames were slowly trying to reach toward the sky through the layers of firewood reminded me of a time when I ran my first 5k race. Being a novice runner, I forced myself to muster every bit of strength I had to make it to the finish line. I saw it in the distance while the surrounding runners, who were clearly not struggling as much as I was, passed me by.

I shrugged my shoulders and sighed with a little smile.

Oh well. Thank God I at least thought to bring this blanket outside.

I picked the soft brown blanket up off the green folding camp chair that was sitting beside the fire pit.

I wrapped the blanket around me, placed my camp chair closer to the tiny fire, picked up my mug of hot tea off the ground, and brushed off the little bit of dirt that clung to the bottom of it. I brought the mug up to my lips, blew into the cup to try to take the edge of heat away, and took a sip.

"Dammit," I said as I burned my tongue slightly. I knew it was still too hot but took a sip anyway—a gamble I take too often.

Late evening was my favorite time to sit down by the fire. As the sun set over the mountains, it left a lingering purple hue as the night sky settled in. Crickets were chirping, and I found myself daydreaming as I looked into the fire, warming my hands with the hot mug as I held it up to my chest.

I turned around and looked behind me, smiling at the tiny cabin that was sitting on top of the little hill. The front porch was lit and there were moths fluttering around the light.

I still can't believe it's mine.

I was so proud of the fact that I was able to finally fulfill my lifelong dream of living in a cabin. I smiled as I turned to look back toward the fire. The dark purple sky was giving way to total darkness. The few twinkling stars that were making their appearances across the vast night sky along with the rustling in the leaves of the trees from the chilled breeze created a perfect sense of peace and contentment. The crackling fire was offering serenity and comfort as the darkness of the night enveloped my surroundings.

"Ms. Mosher?"

What was that?

I wanted to turn around and look at where the noise was coming from but instead, I stared straight ahead.

Am I hearing things? I am alone in the middle of nowhere. I didn't hear anyone walking up to me. Surely I would have heard something like footsteps or the snapping sound of twigs breaking under the pressure of someone's body weight.

I reassured myself it was probably just the wind. Or maybe it was a ghost! I laughed because I believe in ghosts, and I entertained myself for a few seconds with that slight possibility.

I felt someone gently tapping my shoulder. "Ms. Mosher?"

Oh no. Did I feel that? Was that real?

I froze. My eyes widened in fear as I stared into the fire, gripping my mug tight with white knuckles. I affixed my eyes on a log resting on the outside of the others that hadn't been fully engulfed in flames yet. I was alone. I had no way to protect myself. As irrational as it sounds, I wanted to grab the log and throw it at whomever the person was. I hesitated, wondering if he or she was innocent. I didn't want to hurt anyone.

Oh my God, what do I do?

At that moment, my mind was racing so fast that all I could do was just freeze. My body was completely numb.

A woman's soft voice asked "Ms. Mosher? Ms. Mosher, can you sit up please?"

I was already sitting up. I was obviously hearing things.

Am I going crazy? Either I'm losing my mind, or I'm being haunted by a seriously sweet-sounding stealthy ghost. I must be going crazy.

The woman shined a bright flashlight into my eyes. I squinted at the light, trying to make sense of my surroundings.

"Huh? What? Wait, where am I?" I asked in confusion. I was starting to panic. The darkness of the woods gave way to a bright room with stark white walls.

"What's going on? I was just at my cabin. Where's the cabin? Where's the fire? Where am I? Who are you?"

"Excuse me, Ms. Mosher, I'm sorry to wake you but I need to take your vital signs again."

Highly confused and exhausted, I slowly sat up. My head was pounding, and it was definitely the worst headache I've ever had. As the nurse gently took my arm to read my blood pressure, I struggled to open my eyes more and slowly turned my head toward her.

It hurt to move. My body felt incredibly weak and weighed down. The lights above me were blindingly white. The delightful smell of the burning wood of my campfire was long gone and was traded in for the agonizing, sharp scents of bleach, stainless steel, and misery.

I looked up into the deep brown eyes of the nurse, pleading with her silently to take me away from whatever that place was. She didn't receive my message though; instead she smiled at me and looked down at her watch. Confused still, my eyes and face felt heavy as my gaze followed hers down to my right wrist where she was gently applying pressure in order to check my pulse.

"Oh no… Oh no…. No, no, no, no," I whispered in desperation, tears forming in my eyes again as I looked at the two wristbands that I was wearing. The smaller white wristband, a symbol of my physical identity with my name and date of birth, was overshadowed by the thick, dark orange wristband with large, bold, capital letters—SUICIDE RISK—a declaration to the world of my new mental identity.

I couldn't believe that it was real.

All of a sudden, I remembered that I was a patient on a seventy-two hour hold in a psychiatric ward. I came dangerously close to death by my own two hands the day before I went into the hospital. The events in my life that led me to that place were replaying in my mind over and over. I was so tired of being scared and living in fear. I was clinging for dear life on the thought that there could be a tiny ray of hope that was buried deep down within me somewhere, praying it would somehow manifest itself and save me. I had never felt more distraught, ashamed, and broken in my entire life.

"Do you still have your headache, Ms. Mosher?" she asked in a comforting and soft-spoken voice as she finished taking my temperature.

"Yes, um, but it's really intense. I- I- Um, I thought it would be gone by now," I struggled to say through the tears.

"It's the withdrawal from the Ativan. Would you like some Tylenol for your headache, Ms. Mosher?"

Embarrassed, I said, "Yes, please."

I thanked her as she handed me a small plastic cup with two Tylenol inside. My hands were shaking, I couldn't stop crying, and I just wanted relief from the physical pain of the headache and the emotional pain of feeling so empty.

I placed the Tylenol in my mouth and took a large sip of room temperature water. I closed my eyes and fought hard to swallow the pills in disgust because the lukewarm water had taken on the acrid flavor of the cup it had been sitting in all night along with an aftertaste of the smell of the hospital room. The taste of the water made me cringe and shudder and the pills were resisting my efforts to swallow.

The nurse gathered all her belongings as I laid back down, burying my head in my hands into a tear-soaked pillow. I just wanted to go back to sleep.

At the time, I would have given anything to go back to that dream and sit next to that fire because it was the most peace I had felt in years. Once I was awakened, I realized that I was back living the horrible nightmare of living a life that was full of fear, pain, sadness, anxiety, loneliness, and extreme heartache. The fear of being abandoned that grew within me over the years had overtaken every aspect of my life to the point where I felt I couldn't handle living with the pain anymore.

CHAPTER TWO

ABANDONED

———

Took you by surprise, huh?

Let's rewind back to 2006 and I'll get you all caught up.

On October 16, a little over four years into our marriage, my husband Joe and I separated. The separation was something that I did not see coming at all. The suddenness of it left me alone with the newfound reality that I was going to be a single mom to my three-year-old daughter, Elora, and my six-month-old infant son, Dylan. It left me distraught, devastated, and traumatized. My anxiety was constantly very high, and it debilitated me.

I'm in this large room but the walls are darkening and narrowing in on me. They are trapping and suffocating me. Why does it feel like I can't take deep breaths? My heart is racing. Panic is pulsating through my body. My veins feel like they are on fire. My stomach hurts so bad, but I can't eat.

The concept of sleep was becoming increasingly foreign due to my mind racing in all sorts of directions with constant cycles of questions scattering throughout my head, like *what's wrong with me? Why am I not good enough for him? Was I not pretty enough? Should I have tried harder to look beautiful or dress nicer? Was I not desirable at all? Is he happier with someone else? What could I have done differently so that he could have been happy with me? I've been a stay-at-home mom for a while and I never finished college, so how am I going to financially take care of myself and two children?*

I knew we got married so young and that there were a lot of responsibilities on his shoulders. I reluctantly accepted that the distance and time apart due to his Navy career wore us down. I was just in shock.

I became obsessed with wondering what I needed to do to fix my physical appearance.

Should I wear more makeup? Should I style my hair differently? What if I dressed nicer? But what's the point? He won't want me back anyway.

The obsession just remained in my thoughts though because I couldn't find the strength to even brush my hair most days.

My self-esteem was shattered, and my confidence was heavily defeated.

For the first two weeks after the separation, it was normal if the only thing I ate most days was half of a Pepperidge Farm Milano cookie. Being petite already, I couldn't afford to lose any weight. I just wasn't hungry. I had two young children who needed me, and it literally took everything I had in me to muster up the strength to make sure they were taken care of. Attempts to sleep would fail nightly, resulting in me sitting on the living room couch just staring absentmindedly out of the dark window. Dylan was still waking up at night to drink a bottle, and if I happened to doze off, he would need to be fed shortly thereafter. I was literally a walking zombie.

I need to see a doctor or something. This anxiety is taking over my life. I hate this lack of control over my body.

I slowly walked into the office with knotted and wildly disheveled hair. Tears welled in my eyes and lightly descended my cheeks, adding moisture and depth to the skin surrounding my eyes that were darkened by the lack of sleep.

What does it matter if I get dressed up anyway? Nobody is going to want me, a 24-year-old woman with all this baggage. I'm going to be alone forever.

"Can you step up on the scale please?"

I stepped up on the scale, completely numb to the world. I was tired and exhausted. I hadn't slept in days.

"This can't be right," the nurse mumbled as she moved the dial back and forth on the scale from zero to one hundred.

"I haven't been able to eat in two weeks," I told her with barely any strength left in me. The number on the scale was quite alarming—eighty-two pounds. Although I was shocked to know that I weighed only eighty-two pounds, the number made sense. Being five foot four, the bones in my chest and hips were protruding and my face was sunken in. I was literally wasting away.

The doctor expressed serious concern for my weight. "You are losing weight fast and I'm concerned that you're malnourished. If you continue to lose weight, we may have to look into hospitalization. Bottom line is you aren't going to be able to fight the anxiety on your own. I think you will benefit from taking an anti-anxiety medication. With the anxiety lessening, your ability to eat can hopefully return." He prescribed me a low dose of Xanax, an anti-anxiety medication to take as needed, and sent me home to my tiny apartment.

...

On the Monday after Thanksgiving, I packed up our belongings, secured Elora and Dylan into their car seats, and prepared to drive north. I started the ignition and looked at my two children in the backseat.

I am so scared of this new life ahead of me but I'm ready to go back home to Pennsylvania. Thank God I have Kristie with me.

"I still can't believe you came down here to help me do this," I said as I stared blankly out the windshield.

"Tiff, that's what best friends are for," Kristie, my best friend since we were three years old, replied as she rubbed my arm gently with her hand. "We're like sisters. We're family."

I closed my eyes and then turned my head toward her. As I opened my eyes and looked into hers, tears started to fall. "Kristie, I don't know if I can do this. I don't know if I can move on from this."

Tears formed in her eyes. "Yes, you can. I know it's scary, but you can, and you will. And when you doubt yourself, just know you have to do it for them," she said as she looked back at Elora and Dylan. She looked back at me. "You have to stay strong for your little ones. And you know I'm here to help you in any way that I can."

I wrapped my arms around her and whispered "thank you" as I hugged her tight. She was my saving grace.

Nine hours later, the kids and I arrived at our new home.

One thing I vowed from the get-go was that when I was ready to date, I would never EVER date a sailor again because 1) the Navy lifestyle was too hard for me to handle and 2) I won't go into details, but I simply didn't find sailors to be trustworthy with my fragile heart.

My parents offered to help me financially for the first few months until I got back on my feet but emotionally, I felt very isolated and alone. I got a job as a Medical Transcriptionist at the local hospital. It felt good to be able to support my little family. However, it was very hard being a single mom. Dylan was still waking up once a night to eat. I worked forty hours a week and didn't get adequate sleep. Financially, I was barely able to live paycheck to paycheck. The kids and I lived off ramen noodles, eggs, and Spaghettios. At one point, I only had ten dollars to my name to last me for an entire week, but I was too embarrassed to ask for help.

I just want to feel accepted by something, by anything, by anyone. I'm desperate. I don't care what it takes. I'm willing to do whatever I can to feel it.

Christmas and New Year's flew by. Starting the new year was not a celebration by any means.

I'm starting this year alone and broke. This year is going to be the worst year, I swear.

On the weekends that I didn't have my kids, all inhibition went out the window. Never being one to fancy the taste of beer, I found comfort in the liquor bottle. I frequented the local bar, Cuz-N-Joe's, and would drink whatever was offered to me. Rum and Coke or Malibu Bay Breezes quickly turned into shots of rum, vodka, and Southern Comfort, or whatever some random guy offered to buy me.

I engaged in unprotected sex. Why? Well, for one, I didn't have any health insurance benefits and couldn't get access to a birth control prescription and two, I just thought the guys would provide the protection.

The dangerous coping strategies of alcohol and sex provided temporary relief but only left me feeling emptier later.

At one point, before Dylan was even one year old, I thought I was pregnant. Having had sex with three different guys that month, again, unprotected, I wouldn't have even known who the father was.

I feel so alone and disgusted with myself. This is a horrible feeling. I don't know what else to do.

CHAPTER THREE

HALF EMPTY, HALF FULL

———

"I'll have another rum and Coke, please."

God, it's only three months into 2007 and it's already the longest and worst year of my life. Last night sucked. I need this drink.

Too embarrassed to discuss what happened the night before with anyone I knew personally, I opted to confide in a stranger the following night at Cuz-N-Joe's after a couple of rum and Cokes. There was a cute, tall, dark-haired guy who looked to be in his mid-thirties and had been sitting alone at the bar for quite some time and hadn't been looking at his phone to text anyone.

I had to do my research, you see, because I was not about to intrude on some other woman's territory. I decided to walk over to him.

"Hi, I'm Tiffany." I extended my hand to the tall, dark-haired guy sitting alone at the bar.

"Ben," he said, shaking my hand in return. "Have a seat. What are you drinking?"

"Rum and Coke, please."

He caught the attention of the bartender. "Two rum and Cokes."

The bartender looked at me, looked down at my glass that was now half empty, shrugged his shoulders, and pulled out two glasses. Ben looked back at me and smiled. "So, how are you?"

"I don't want to get into that right now," I said dismissively, waving my hand in the air a little bit. The one and a half rum and Cokes that I already drank had kicked in, and I felt a buzz coming on. "Are you a cop?" I asked him confidently.

"Um, no, why?" he asked, obviously very confused.

"So, you aren't a cop. Can I ask you something then?"

He looked at me as if he was thinking "what the fuck did I get myself into?" "Uhhh..." he said hesitantly.

"I just need someone to talk to. Someone that's not a cop."

"Okay, well, I'm not a cop. So, what do you need to talk about? Are you on the run or something?"

"Jesus, no, nothing like that," I said in an offended tone.

"Okay, sorry," he said as he put his hands up in surrender. "What is it then?"

"What do you know about date rape drugs?"

"Excuse me?" He laughed in a confused way. "Nothing, I know nothing. I swear."

"Bullshit. I'm serious. I need advice."

"I don't have any on me and I don't know any dealers," he said with caution.

"That's not what I'm needing advice about. I kind of think I was drugged with something. I think there was something mixed in with my drink."

"What? When, just now?" he asked, showing a tiny bit of concern.

"No, last night."

"Okay, so you're saying you were possibly drugged last night?"

"I guess?" I asked, shrugging my shoulders while looking down at my drink and swirling the straw around the glass uncomfortably.

"I'm guessing that I can assume that something bad happened to you, huh?"

"Yeah."

"If you'd like to share, I'm willing to listen and see how I can help."

"Okay, um, well, I was hanging out with a 'friend' who offered me a drink. A little while after I finished the drink, my surroundings went completely dark. The only colors I could see were black and white. Timing was very spacey, kind of like a strobe light effect. I felt like I was in a haunted house or something. And strangely, I had absolutely no control over myself. I remember being downstairs in my basement, completely clothed, and then the next thing I knew I was naked upstairs in my bedroom with him naked on my bed. I literally have no idea what happened. Like, I'm sure we had sex–he said we did– but I don't remember it at all. Not a thing."

"Oh shit."

"Yeah."

"Okay. I never had anything like that happen to me before, but my guess is your drink was definitely drugged with something. Maybe PCP? Don't quote me on that though."

"PCP? What's PCP?"

"Angel dust."

"Ugh," I said, burying my head in my hands. "So, if my friend got me high on this PCP or whatever, does that mean that the sex was consensual?"

He turned toward me, placed his hands on my shoulders, and looked into my eyes. "First of all, Tiffany, whoever this was person was that willingly gave that to you is not your friend. You know that right?"

"I know that now."

"Second, no, the sex was not consensual if you don't remember it. Are you okay? Are you hurt?" he asked genuinely.

I started to tear up. "Yes, I'm okay. No, I'm not hurt."

"Why are you crying?" He offered me a bar napkin.

"Because I feel like a piece of shit for allowing this to happen."

"Would you like advice from a random stranger you just met in a bar?"

"Yes, please."

"My advice is choose your friends wisely. Stay away from shit like that. Focus on the good things that are going on in your life."

"I know."

"I have to go, but I'm going to say one more thing before I do. Between you and me, you're a beautiful woman. You have so much potential. And my name isn't Ben. It's Aaron. I've seen you around here a few times. I could sense that you are having a hard time with something. Look, whatever it is, it isn't my business. Don't take this the wrong way, but at the end of the day, you need to love and respect yourself. Please be careful."

He's seen me acting promiscuous around here before. How embarrassing!

I felt ashamed and looked down at the floor.

"That was in no way to offend you. Just some advice from one new friend to another."

"Why did you tell me your name is Ben?"

"Because I wasn't sure of your intentions in talking to me. Just playing it safe, that's all. I apologize."

"It's okay, I understand. Thank you for listening though, really. I appreciate it."

We gave each other a quick side hug. He patted me on the back and walked out the door. I looked around the bar hoping to see a familiar face, but I couldn't find anyone I knew. I couldn't drive home yet because of how much I drank so I ordered some water and waited awhile.

I used the time for some mental reflection. I knew I needed to find a better way to cope with my abandonment issues or else these careless acts would eventually kill me. I felt like a horrible person and a terrible mother. I loved my children, I really did. I just couldn't keep hiding from the pain anymore. I needed to face my struggles head on.

Over the next two months, I tried very hard to keep an open mind when it came to dating and to not assume that all guys were horrible. Although I never saw Aaron around Cuz-N-Joe's again, the conversation that we had that night led to me believe that maybe there were still some good guys out there.

Maybe, just maybe, there's someone out there for me. I want to find love and be able to trust someone again.

...

In May 2007, I started dating Alex.

Oh God, he's in the Navy too. I guess that goes against my pact of "never EVER dating a sailor again."

We had known each other as acquaintances for about three years and reconnected on Myspace. I got lost in his deep brown eyes immediately and when he accepted my children and I as a package deal, I felt as if I had to hold onto him for dear life because who else would have wanted me?

Alex and I were the epitome of the phrase "opposites attract." He is very spontaneous; I am an avid planner. He is a night owl; I am an early bird. He has difficulty remembering important dates and appointments; my mind is a calendar. He loves coffee; I love tea. He loves peanut butter; I absolutely hate it. You get the idea. The point is that we counterbalanced each other beautifully.

He left for a deployment six months after we started dating and I quickly adjusted back to the Navy lifestyle. In February 2008, he was ordered to a base in Maryland. The kids and I moved down to that area from Pennsylvania and we started our life together. Our relationship was solid and strong, and the time spent apart seemed to help us grow closer together. Elora and Dylan adored him. We got engaged in May 2008 and had a secret courthouse wedding a few months later.

In May 2009, just four days prior to a wedding ceremony we had planned for family and friends, I found out I was pregnant again.

Oh my God, am I ready for this? Baby number three? I'm never going to sleep again!

I was excited at first but then I got scared because I wasn't sure if I was in the right place in my life to have another child. I was also scared that Alex was going to abruptly leave, and I would be left having to care for three children instead of two. I had already experienced being a single parent before and I didn't think I could make it through all of that again. I felt kind of stuck but decided to change my mindset and make the most of things.

Still living in constant fear of the unknown and wanting to find something to distract myself, I decided to enroll at the University of Maryland to pursue my bachelor's degree in Social Science. I chose Social Science at the time because it was a broad degree and I still had no idea what I wanted to do with my life yet. I just felt compelled to start somewhere and I hoped I would just figure out a plan along the way.

I took a Cultural Anthropology class as one of my required courses for the program, and immediately fell in love with the subject. Learning about different cultures around the world was fascinating and I could not stop researching various types of indigenous societies. After that course, I decided to concentrate on anthropology and sociology.

On a bitter cold January morning in 2010, I gave birth to a baby boy named Mason. After only three hours of labor, I became a mother to three children, and it was an intimidating yet incredible feeling. A few months after Mason's birth, we relocated to Virginia Beach due to Alex's new orders with the Navy.

I'm so tired of moving. I just want to stay somewhere for a while.

In January 2011, Alex left for a six-month deployment. We did our best to maintain communication via e-mail and through occasional phone calls. Things were going well, but when he returned from the deployment there was an unsettling feeling because another deployment was on the horizon nine months later. With deployments, it was a normal feeling to want to emotionally detach from each other because it was easier to say goodbye for an extended period of time if our hearts were guarded.

Anxiety played tricks on my own mind which caused me to try to purposefully find character flaws in Alex when they didn't really exist. I searched for anything and everything that could be wrong.

He's running late from work and hasn't called yet. Is he with someone else?

He didn't give me any affection today. Is something wrong with me? Does he not want to spend time with me?

My actions emotionally drained both of us. He was so patient, knowing I had been through the trauma of a difficult divorce before and wanted to try to appease my mind. I depended on his validation for everything in order to be happy. I needed constant affirmation, constant communication, and could only feel emotionally safe when he was physically around me.

In March 2012, Alex left for an eight-month deployment. I continued with my bachelor's degree to keep my mind occupied. Studying helped give me a sense of purpose and I earned As in most of my courses. Although things were going well, worry and paranoia crept into my thoughts because he was going to be gone for so long.

Don't dwell in the happiness. Something bad is going to happen at some point. Be paranoid. Stay afraid.

Trust in your fear, Tiffany, so you can be mentally prepared for anything that comes your way.

CHAPTER FOUR

THE DEVIL'S DOORSTEP

───

Check me out in this cap and gown! It took me thirteen long and difficult years, but it's finally here! It's graduation day!

The following year in May 2013, I finally graduated with my bachelor's degree. The purple and yellow honors society ropes that adorned my neck added an exquisite brightness to the black of my cap and gown.

I entered the Comcast Center at the University of Maryland, College Park, and tears filled my eyes as the bright shining lights along with the applause of the thousands of families and friends of my fellow graduates greeted us. Alex, my children, my parents and stepparents, my mother-in-law, and some of my aunts and uncles were in attendance. It felt so good to have their support and see them in the stands cheering me on. I graduated *magna cum laude,* and I wore the garments with pride.

I pushed myself through divorce, multiple pregnancies, and the Navy lifestyle. I worked so hard to succeed and achieve good grades. I felt proud of myself that day. I received a degree in a subject I was passionate about.

I don't know what I'm going to do with this degree, but man I love anthropology and sociology. I can't wait to start my dream job! I don't know what it is yet, but still! I feel like such an adult now! Bring on the money!

The joy, though, quickly turned into confusion and possible regret. I was questioned by some family members and friends on why I would want to pay for a degree in a field that did not pay well.

"You know you aren't going to make any real kind of money with a degree in a field like that, right?"

"Why didn't you choose something that is relevant to the world today?"

"Are you sure you picked the right field? Why didn't you choose business or something cool like engineering?"

Way to kick a girl down when she's feeling good, right? But these were the true winners:

"Isn't getting a degree in Social Science basically like getting a degree in basket weaving?"

"What is anthropology, anyway? Isn't that when they dig up dinosaur bones? Are you going to act like you're in *Jurassic Park* or something?"

Seriously? Give me a freaking break. I love studying the subjects. Big deal. No, I'm not going to be digging up dinosaur bones. But whatever. Doesn't it make more sense to spend the money on studying something I enjoy learning about?

I applied for over two hundred jobs but never had any luck landing one interview. I became discouraged and started to believe that what everyone was saying was right.

Maybe I did choose the wrong course of study.

I loved the field of anthropology though. Learning about different cultural practices around the world was so fascinating. Whether it was my family members, friends, or someone that I just met and was having a casual conversation with asked me what anthropology was, I would get excited to talk about the indigenous cultural studies that fascinated me. However, more often than not I would receive a sarcastic "oh, well that's cool" response. The more opposition I received, the more I felt like a failure.

Why doesn't anyone want to understand what makes me happy? I know anthropology is different. Why can't I enjoy it?

Over time, those negative feelings of shame, along with the anxiety that consumed me in my marriage, progressively caused my sharp decline into depression the following summer. I felt worthless and that I had no purpose. I felt like I wasted my time and money on a pointless degree. I was sad all the time and tried begging Alex for his help, but my depression was hard for him to deal with. My depression made him uncomfortable because he had never dealt with it before.

His keeping me at arms-length increased my fear of abandonment even more because I felt that I was going to be too much to handle and that he was going to leave me. I knew I was hard to deal with but had no clue how to change my mindset. I was scared all the time. The thoughts of possible impending loneliness that I manifested within myself consumed me, and I honestly believed that I wouldn't be able to handle the constant worrying anymore. I needed to take matters into my own hands to feel somewhat in control of my emotions.

My sadness and sense of worthlessness continued to grow over time. I found it increasingly hard to find any sort of joy in anything.

...

One year later in May 2014, after a weekend visiting with my in-laws, we were heading home and drove across the Harry W. Nice Memorial Bridge on Route 301 at the Maryland/

Virginia border. Alex was driving and as the passenger, I stared out the window as we crossed over the bridge. I found myself fantasizing about what it would feel like to stand on the edge of that bridge, looking up at the blue sky with my shoulder-length brown hair and dark blue ankle-length sundress softly blowing in the wind.

How peaceful would it feel to just spread my arms out wide, close my eyes, and release my body from the bridge's edge, plunging down toward the river below to my death? Would it hurt? What would it feel like? Would I die on impact or would I suffer in pain and drown?

None of that mattered though because at least I wouldn't be in emotional pain anymore.

I fully believed that nobody would even care if I was gone.

One sunny Saturday morning, Alex, the kids, and I were out running errands. I honestly didn't want to go because I woke up very sad and unmotivated that morning, as was the usual way I woke up most days. While we were driving to the grocery store, I looked out the window and became hypnotized by the trees and buildings blurring past.

Alex must have noticed my melancholy stature and asked me out of nowhere, "Hey, I have an idea. What's something that reminds you of something good? Like a song or something positive from your childhood?"

Already annoyed because I just didn't want to think of anything happy at that point, I shrugged my shoulders. "I don't know."

"C'mon, there has to be something. You can look it up on YouTube and we can plug in the aux cord and play it while we drive. Maybe that will help you."

An idea came to mind, but it felt absolutely ridiculous. "Well, back when I was in high school, at one of my regional band festivals, we played this piece called 'Gandalf, the Wizard.' You know, like from the movie *The Lord of the Rings*. Anyway, it was my favorite piece that I ever played. It's just, I don't know, so powerful, and there was one part that gave me goosebumps." I started to laugh and smile.

"I remember during rehearsals, my friend Stephanie and I would get so excited for that part of the song and we would gently nudge each other when it was about to happen. For the main performance, they took video of the entire concert and during 'Gandalf, the Wizard' they actually caught us nudging each other and smiling at each other. I'll never forget that."

"Did you just notice that?" he asked me.

"Notice what?"

"You smiled and laughed when you told that story. Look it up. See if you can find it, let's listen to it."

"It's an orchestra piece though. You don't like orchestra music."

"Whatever. It's fine. Look it up!"

I started to search YouTube and for the life of me I could not remember who the composer was. After a quick Google search, I went onto YouTube and searched "Gandalf, the Wizard Johan de Meij" and I was surprised to see that there were many videos to choose from. I clicked on the first video and nervously waited for the ads to finish playing. As the song began to play, I recognized the opening sequence of the vibrant horns and percussion.

"Oh my God, this is it. This is it!" Tears formed in my eyes immediately. I looked out of the window while resting my head against the back of the gray leather seat, listening to this magical piece that I hadn't heard in many years. Despite the trees and buildings and world around me flying past so quickly, time seemed to just slow down to a halt. The sounds of the horns and woodwinds immediately took me back to my junior year, sitting within the orchestra, where I felt the most successful in my life. For those brief moments, I was a musician again. I had talent once again.

Performing this piece brought me so much joy and passion. It starts off strong and bold portraying J.R.R. Tolkien's vision of the mystical wizard Gandalf the Grey with his long hair and beard. Then, about two minutes in, the tempo picks up symbolizing Gandalf and his horse, Shadowfax, galloping through the forest and across the countryside.

Then came my favorite part. At around the 3:38 mark, the music slows down dramatically and builds up into this magnificent display of percussion, horns, and woodwinds that symbolizes when Gandalf the Grey transitioned to Gandalf the White after his courageous battle with the demon Balrog. The strength and magnitude in the sound of the horns were what gave me chills every time we rehearsed it.

Playing the clarinet, I sat in front of the horn and percussion sections and to hear the intensity of the music was simply breathtaking. Playing that piece was one of the most memorable experiences I ever had as a musician.

Clutching the door handle with white knuckles and tears streaming down my face, I was reminded of a time in my life when I felt full of life, energy, talent, and purpose. For those few minutes, I felt so much happiness. However, after the song ended, I felt sorrow and pain once again.

Where did that girl go? What happened to me? How did I get to this point of feeling so low, broken, and empty? Did motherhood and circumstances of life evolve me so much that I really lost touch with who I used to be? Where did my drive and motivation go? Would I ever find happiness and a sense of achievement again?

It all seemed too far out of reach.

...

Over time, I started to slowly withdraw physically and emotionally from everyone around me. I stopped calling my family and friends and I lost touch with Kristie. I would retreat to my bedroom to hide away from Alex and the kids because I just wanted to be alone all the time. It was just mentally exhausting to be around people.

Maybe medication will help? I'm willing to try anything at this point.

I decided to see a psychiatrist. The psychiatrist diagnosed me with depression and anxiety disorder and over a two-month period, I tried several cocktails of medications that caused weird side effects.

The first cocktail, consisting of Prozac, Lipitor, and Ativan made me nauseous all the time. The next cocktail–Prozac, Abilify, and Ativan–left me feeling flighty and spaced out and unable to recollect periods of time. This was especially dangerous when I would be driving somewhere and not remember how I got there, which happened multiple times. I was then prescribed Risperdal and Ativan, which caused lactation, and was a really weird and dangerous side effect because while it was nice that my boobs got a little bigger, I certainly was not nursing a child at the time.

She finally prescribed me Geodon and Ativan, and that was when more frequent suicidal ideations began. The ideations, consisting of fantasies about how I could take my own life or wanting to be killed, haunted me, and gave me even more anxiety.

I grew to really rely on the Ativan to combat my anxiety. It calmed the pain that surged through my veins and relaxed me. I was prescribed a low dose of Ativan (0.5 mg) and was supposed to only take it when I needed to, but no more than two or three tablets per day. Although I fantasized of death, the concept still made me nervous. I started taking Ativan more often than I should. Sometimes I would take between ten and twelve tablets a day. Thoughts of suicide started to come more frequently, and I was desperate to not feel the pain anymore.

On a cool and rainy Friday night in early October, I had an entire bottle of Ativan in my hand; a whole new prescription that had just been refilled. Alex was sleeping on the couch downstairs, which was something that was becoming more common those days. His wanting to sleep apart from me rightfully triggered my fear of abandonment.

I should just kill myself in my bedroom. That'll teach him a harsh lesson.

My plan was to just take them all, fall asleep, and never wake up. As I was about to swallow the pills, a feeling within me told me to go check on Mason. I compromised that I would take the pills as soon as I made sure he and the other kids were all okay and asleep.

I first checked on Elora and Dylan, and then went into Mason's room. He must have sensed me in there because he opened his eyes and looked up at me.

"Hi Mama," he said, reaching his arms out to me with half-opened eyes.

I realized at that moment that I wasn't ready to die quite yet. I picked him up carefully and carried him into my bedroom so that he could sleep with me for the rest of the night. I rubbed his back and watched him until he fell into a peaceful slumber. Little did he know that having him there beside me, my sweet and innocent four-year-old baby boy, was what kept me alive that night.

I woke up the next day feeling like a zombie with zero emotion, like a stone. I went through the motions of the day but continued to feel empty and to just feel nothing, in part thanks to the Ativan.

Two days later, all three kids were watching *SpongeBob SquarePants* on television. I was washing dishes at the kitchen sink, which looked into the living room. As I washed the dishes, I picked up the large chef's knife that I had used to chop tomatoes, cucumbers, and lettuce for the salad we ate with our dinner an hour prior. The water was a little too hot and added a slight burning sensation to my hands. I slid the soapy sponge up and down the knife's edge. I began to fantasize about what it would feel like to insert the sharp blade into my wrist and forearm.

I can end the pain right here, right now.

I held the knife to my wrist, applied pressure, and closed my eyes.

Right then, a haunting image abruptly flashed before my eyes of my pale and ghostly white body lying motionless in a massive amount of bright red blood with my eyes open, staring up straight ahead but with no life left in them. Absolutely terrified, I opened my eyes quickly in a panic and threw the knife as hard as I could down into the sink. The impact of the knife hitting a drinking glass caused the glass to shatter. Wide-eyed and trembling profusely, I started to cry and breathe deeply.

"Mom? What happened?" Dylan asked, as he and Elora looked back at me, wondering what all the commotion was about.

"Um, oh, I just dropped something by mistake, buddy."

"Why are you crying? Did you get hurt?"

I wiped the tears from my eyes and wiped my nose. "No, no I'm not hurt. I, um, just thought of something sad for a second. Mommy's fine, don't worry."

"What do you mean you thought of something sad?"

I needed to come up with a response fast. "Oh, you know, uh, I just miss my family back home in Pennsylvania. Grammy, Grandpop, Grandmom, my aunts and uncles, you know, all my family. I haven't seen them in a while."

"But we just saw Grandpop at Disney World in the summertime." That was true. We took a big family vacation to Disney World in July and we all had a great time together as a family.

"Yes buddy, that's true, but I still miss my family."

"Okay."

The kids turned their attention back toward the television. I did miss my family so damn much. I was all alone in Virginia Beach with my closest family members over an eight-hour drive away. I felt homesick, so incredibly homesick. I was tired of doing everything alone.

I grabbed my Ativan bottle, turned around and slinked down onto the floor. Sobbing heavily, I swallowed two pills to combat the anxiety. I forced myself to take deep breaths. The bloody vision was still haunting me.

The next morning, I took a shower and blow-dried my hair. Then I was going to flat-iron it because my hair had a mind of its own and if I didn't flat-iron it, my hair would be a curly and frizzy mess. I sat down at my vanity in my bedroom and pulled the flat iron out of the drawer. Alex was in the shower that was less than ten feet away from me, right on the other side of the wall that I was facing. I could hear the water running. As I sat and looked at the mirror and stared into my own eyes, I felt absolute disgust at what I saw. All I saw was ugliness.

There isn't even one beautiful thing about me anymore. My reflection is downright repulsive.

"Look at you," I whispered out loud to myself, as I picked up the flat iron, staring intently into my own eyes in the mirror. "You are a failure. What can you honestly say you've done with your life?"

I looked down at the cord and started to stretch it out slowly, intertwining it in between my fingers. I slowly brought my eyes back up to the mirror. I raised my voice slightly. "Nothing. You've done nothing meaningful but drive your marriage into failure because you can't handle your damn emotions." I slowly wrapped the cord once around my neck. I was looking at what I felt was pure genuine evil.

I clenched my teeth, glaring into my own eyes intently as if I was forcing what was left of my soul directly into the darkness and depths of hell. "You are nothing but an ugly piece of shit." I wrapped the cord once more around my neck tightly. "Nobody wants you here. Go ahead. Do it! The world's better off without you in it anyway."

I slowly started to pull the cord tight from both sides. I welcomed the pain at the start of the strangulation. I continued to stare at myself, my face getting red, hating what I saw, just wishing it was all over. My surroundings started fading into darkness.

All of a sudden, Alex shut the shower water off and it pulled me out of the crazy trance I was in.

"Oh my God! Oh my God, what am I doing?" I looked around in confusion. The water had shut off at the right time. It was another sign presented to me, but this time, it hit me the hardest because I was so terribly close to ending my life.

"Oh my God, I don't want to die. I can't do this. I can't do this!" It was true. I didn't want to die. I wanted to try to live. I wanted to find purpose.

Knowing Alex was about to come out of the bathroom any second, I unwrapped the cord from around my neck. I wanted to be there for my kids. They needed me. I was suffering, and I was so unbelievably tired of feeling that way. My depression and anxiety were too much for me to fight on my own. I needed help.

Alex came out of the bathroom. I looked up and stared at him with immense fear, wide eyes, quivering lips, and tears pouring down my face.

"What's wrong? Are you okay?" he asked me in a panic.

"No." I sobbed heavily.

"What happened? Oh shit, why is your neck all red?"

I held up the flat iron and the cord and he knew exactly what that meant.

"I need help. Please help me!" I cried and begged, desperate at this point for anything that would help. He grabbed the flat iron out of my hands and threw it onto the floor behind him. He picked me up off the chair, hugged me tight, and then called a suicide hotline number. They suggested that he take me to the emergency room.

I had officially hit rock bottom. I knew something had to change or I wouldn't be alive much longer. Handling my depression on my own didn't work. Medication didn't work. The changing of my physical surroundings over the years due to military moves didn't work. Leaning on others to build me back up didn't work.

What is it going to take for me to be strong again? What is the secret to being happy?

Humbled and ready to accept help, I voluntarily admitted myself to the hospital for psychiatric evaluation.

CHAPTER FIVE

HOPE SPRINGS ETERNAL

———

That was quite heavy, wasn't it?

Now that you are all caught up on the bac story of what led to my depression and ultimately to being in a psychiatric hospital, let's dive back in to where we left off.

"Ms. Mosher, time for breakfast."

I opened my eyes slightly and looked toward the door. There was a silhouette of a body in the door frame. I was still so tired.

"Okay, um, what time is it?"

The person in the doorway sighed heavily. "It's 5:30 a.m." The woman's voice sounded annoyed like I was inconveniencing her by having to answer my question.

"Okay, I'm getting up."

With my eyes still closed, I rolled over to my left and slid my hand across the bedside table to find my glasses. I slowly opened the temples of my glasses and placed them on my face. After opening my eyes slowly, I looked over toward the window and saw nothing but darkness. The sun had not yet presented itself to the world.

I turned my head slowly and stared up at the ceiling. I could tell that my hair was a knotted mess from the wetness of the tears and tossing and turning all night. The dream I had the night before–the dream about my little campfire and living in a cabin–felt so real. I remembered every detail so vividly.

Well, now I'm stuck in this depressing and dreary hospital. Why did that nurse have to wake me up and ruin that moment for me?

As I tried to sit up in my bed, I noticed that the Tylenol had provided a tiny bit of relief from my headache. I slid the blankets off me and planted my feet onto the floor. The withdrawal from all the Ativan had taken a toll on me. My whole body was achy and sore even though I hadn't exerted myself physically. I walked carefully toward the door in my oversized brown scrubs and poked my head around the corner of the doorway. The other psychiatric patients that were wearing the same clothing seemed just as tired and worn down as I was. I walked toward the tables they were sitting at eating their breakfast and took a seat that was isolated from everyone else.

"Your breakfast, Ms. Mosher."

"Thank you," I replied, looking down at my tray.

The menu I filled out the night prior was tucked underneath my chocolate milk, the pencil markings from my meal choices smudged from the condensation of the carton. I stared blankly at my tray and without moving my head, looked cautiously at the people around me. Everyone was eating and some were drinking coffee.

I hate coffee. Actually, I despise the taste of it, and I am not about to start drinking it now.

I pulled out my menu, read over it, rolled my eyes, and tossed it back down. I was in disbelief that tea wasn't on the menu.

Like seriously, what the fuck? What kind of hospital is this?

The last thing I wanted to do was eat. However, I forced down my oatmeal, fruit cup, and chocolate milk. After eating, I joined the other patients, standing in a line to get my vital signs checked yet again. Every move I made was being watched and I felt like I was under constant scrutiny by the staff. There was no essence of privacy, but I knew it was the job of the nurses and doctors to keep me safe.

After all, I did almost commit suicide and that's why I'm here, right?

I had to find something to occupy my time or I was literally going to go crazy (no pun intended). The only real fun thing we could do was read. We were confined to congregate in a main area that had couches and large chairs. I found a corner of a brown leather couch that wasn't occupied and sat down. I had only been there for twenty-four hours and I was already bored out of my mind.

I looked around the room for the hundredth time because maybe, just maybe, something new would present itself. It's kind of like that feeling of when you keep going back into the refrigerator and hope that new food will magically appear that you hadn't seen before. It never works, but we never fail to try it.

Behind me and to the right was the nurse's station, a pharmacy, and a room with a large conference table. Directly to my right, there was an EXIT sign above the door. Next to the nurse's station, there was a thick red line on the floor that us patients were not allowed to cross out of fear of being a flight risk. It was another reminder of the lack of control I had in my life at the time. I rolled my eyes and shook my head slightly at the thought of it.

To my left, there was a hallway that led to our hospital rooms. Ahead of me was a bookshelf that had a bunch of books on it. Some of them seemed new but most of them looked very used with their covers faint and partially torn. The selection was quite limited because the staff could only allow books that wouldn't emotionally trigger the patients. I had looked at that shelf so many times before but, in that moment, there happened to be a book that caught my attention because it was sticking out at an angle more than the other books. My curiosity was sparked in a good way for the first time in a while.

I stood up and tightened the strings of my pants. My dark brown scrubs were so large that I had to constantly adjust them so either my chest wasn't exposed or to prevent my pants from falling down. I literally looked like a giant piece of shit walking around that place. I went over to the shelf and pulled the book out while sliding my fingers across the lightly ripped pages and worn white binding.

I shrugged my shoulders. *What the hell, I have nothing else better to do anyway. Let's see what this one is about.*

Upon reading the title, my heart started racing and I almost dropped the book; it was called *The Journey from Abandonment to Healing* by Susan Anderson.

What are the odds that THIS book is sticking out weirdly on the shelf right now? I looked at this bookshelf so many times and never saw it sticking out before.

Being one to believe in signs and fate, I knew deep down that there had to be a reason that this book caught my attention.

I quickly walked back over to the couch I was sitting on and placed the book down in the corner spot, ensuring nobody else would take my seat. I was really craving some hot tea. I was so nervous but decided to ask for some. I walked up to the nurse's station and patiently waited until I was invited to approach.

"What can I do for you, Ms. Mosher?"

"I was wondering if you have any hot tea?"

The nurse, a young male with dirty blonde wavy hair and who couldn't possibly be any older than twenty-five, was looking at me skeptically. "Hot tea?" he asked, with emphasis on the word hot.

"Yes. I noticed you had coffee this morning but not any tea. I was just going to read for a little bit and thought I would…"

"We can get you something cold like water or a Cola or something to drink."

It's 9:00 a.m. He's offering me a "Cola," really? Who even calls it "Cola" anyway?

Confused and borderline annoyed, I asked, "Oh, so you don't have any hot tea?"

"No, sorry."

Not fully believing him at all and thinking he was purely trying to inconvenience me, I just accepted that I was going to have to wait until I got home to drink some hot tea. I started to walk back to the couch.

"Ms. Mosher?"

"Yes?" I turned around to see where the voice was coming from. I saw a woman in her early forties with her hair pulled back into beautiful long braids calling me over from the pharmacy room with her contagious smile.

I recognize her from somewhere… Ah yes, she's the same nurse that woke me up out of my dream to take my vital signs in the middle of the night.

She motioned for me to come over to her. "Did I hear you ask for some hot tea?"

"Yes, but the male nurse over there said they didn't have any."

"I have an extra tea bag that I brought with me in my lunchbox today."

I automatically got excited. "Oh, really?"

She looked at me with concern. Quietly, she told me, "Look, I'm willing to give you this tea bag but my concern is that the hot water from the staff coffee machine can be really hot."

"Okay?" I asked, looking at her with equal concern, wondering why she was telling me this very common-sense news.

"I'll get you some hot water, but you have to promise me that you won't hurt yourself with it."

Talk about a blow to my ego. I was immediately offended but then quickly resigned to the fact that she had every right to be skeptical of me. After all, it was her job to protect me since I was still deemed to be a "suicide risk."

Tears forming in my eyes, I pleaded with her. "I promise I won't hurt myself. Please believe me. I'll even sit where you can see me drink it at all times. If it makes you feel better, you can let the water cool down to an appropriate temperature of whatever you think is okay before you give it to me. Just please, this cup of tea is just something I really need right now. I need to feel something normal. I just want to feel normal again."

She looked at me with her comforting deep brown eyes. "I believe you, but I'm still going to keep an eye on you. It's for your safety, Ms. Mosher."

"Thank you so, so much," I told her with a smile and appreciative eyes. She made the tea and handed it to me. I could sense she was still skeptical, almost like she was hoping and praying I didn't make her out to be a fool for giving it to me. The water was still hot, so it felt good that she somewhat trusted me.

It felt amazing to hold a hot cup of tea in my hands again. I sat down on the couch next to the book and pulled my knees up to my chest. I held the tea up to my lips, blew into the water to cool it down, and closed my eyes to take a sip.

My eyes widened as I proceeded to burn my tongue a little bit. The nurse was still watching me cautiously from behind the pharmacy counter.

Whatever you do, don't say dammit out loud! Just smile and nod. Smile and nod.

After I drank some of the tea, I opened the book. It was obviously a motivational self-help book and I figured I might as well scan through to see if anything resonated with me. I opened the book to a random page and gasped. The first words that popped out to me were on a list: "A little girl grieving over the death of her mother." I looked up at the name of the list and it was appropriately titled "What is Abandonment?"[3]

I was shocked and disturbed. Those feelings turned to immense frustration with myself because I realized, for the first time, that the one thing that I feared most and struggled with, that fear of abandonment, that fear that drug me down into a pit of despair, the one thing I was running away from and came so close to leaving this world to not feel the pain of anymore, would be the exact thing that I would pass onto Elora, Dylan, and Mason if I were to commit suicide. I would cause that fear to manifest in my innocent children, recreating a vicious cycle.

I wouldn't wish this pain, fear, and sense of hopelessness on anyone, and I was too blind to see that my actions would cause that. I need to find a way to overcome that fear, or at least find a way to handle it better. This message that was sent to me, this sign, couldn't have been more perfect. I needed to see this.

After that awakening, I felt a sense of renewal. My headache had been slowly decreasing throughout the morning, so

---

3   "Excerpt from *The Journey from Abandonment to Healing: Revised and Updated*," Penguin Random House Canada, accessed May 30, 2020.

I figured I would take a shower and approach the rest of my day with a more positive attitude. The shower water was so warm, and the water pressure was borderline perfect. I quickly washed my hair and body because I wanted to just stand in there and enjoy the warmth along with the few minutes of privacy that I could finally have.

I couldn't help but cry because I was happy to be alive. I had taken so much of my life for granted. Even something as simple as a warm shower or the cup of tea I had earlier were things that could bring a sense of peace for a few minutes. I had taken the kindness Alex offered me and the many precious moments spent with my kids for granted.

How did I allow myself to get so deep into despair to the point that I actually thought I would be better off dead? Why did I do that to myself? I really do have a life that's worth living. My kids deserve to have the best mom in the world who is attentive and present, and I have failed them because of my isolation from the world. I have to do better. I wish I could just go home and help Elora and Dylan get ready for school. I wish I could just snuggle with Mason on the couch while we watch a morning cartoon together after we take his siblings to the bus stop. I'm just ready to go home.

Evening visiting hours arrived. I saw Alex checking in at the front desk near the entrance of the psych ward. I walked up close to the thick red line on the floor, but I did not dare to cross it. He was looking over and smiling at me while he waited for a visitor badge. I could sense the sympathy in his eyes. It felt nice yet embarrassing at the same time. It was good to see him, but I looked like a train wreck. My hair, having a mind of its own, air-dried into a frizzy and somewhat curled, somewhat straight mess. My eyes were still puffy and swollen from all the crying.

Pull yourself together, Tiffany.

We sat down across from one another at a table. He smiled at me. "You look beautiful."

"You are such a liar," I immediately said, looking down at my scrubs while trying to flatten my crazy hair. I didn't believe him. *Me? Beautiful? Not looking like this. No way in hell.*

"It's true. You also look like an Ewok straight out of *Star Wars.*"

"Oh my God." I had no choice but to roll my eyes and bury my head in my hands and giggle. He was 100 percent right; I did look like an Ewok. I found myself laughing, and it was nice to somewhat make light of that situation. He always had quick wit and tried to make me laugh. At times, it drove me absolutely crazy. At that moment, I welcomed it. It was exactly what I needed.

...

"Ms. Mosher, how are you feeling today?" a tall, thin, balding man with Harry Potter-type round glasses that were clearly too big for his head asked me.

Who are all these people? This is so embarrassing. Why do I have to miss group therapy for this?

I was sitting in a conference room at the head of the table. There were five other men and women at the table, all staff from the hospital. Before I got brought into the conference room, I was in a group therapy session with other patients. We were taking turns sharing our stories.

"I'm feeling much better this morning, thank you."

"Do you have any feelings of wanting to hurt yourself?"

"No, sir. I want to live. I really do." I recounted the events from the day before with the epiphany I had when I saw the book on the bookshelf.

"Good, that's good," he stated slowly as he flipped through my file.

"Ms. Mosher, my name is Megan Bailey and I'm one of the clinical psychologists here. How would you feel about participating in outpatient rehabilitation?"

"Do you mean like rehab?"

"In a way. It's a day program that you would attend. It will involve intensive individual counseling and group therapy sessions."

"Oh, wow. Um, well, I'm a mom and I have three young children at home. I don't have anyone to watch them during the day for me while I would be at the program and I can't afford daycare. Do I have any other options? I really do want to stay in counseling."

"I understand. Do you feel that if you were to continue counseling sessions with your psychiatrist, that would be enough support for you?"

"Yes, that will be good and much better for my schedule at home with the kids."

Mr. or Dr. Big Harry Potter Glasses flipped back and forth between two pages. "Ms. Mosher, I'm Dr. Kistlenien."

Okay, so it's Dr. Big Harry Potter Glasses. Got it.

"Your chart shows the different combinations of medications that your psychiatrist, Dr. Devitt, prescribed to you."

"Yeah, but I had different weird reactions to them."

"I see that. Are you interested in continuing medication? We can look into some other options for you."

"Well, honestly, I don't know. I am willing to hear what options you have. The thought of it just makes me nervous."

"That's understandable. We will discuss some options with Dr. Devitt."

"Thank you, sir."

After the meeting, I was escorted back to group therapy. Hearing the stories of the other patients was eye-opening and enabled me to look at my situation from a different perspective. *I'm not alone in my struggles. And why do the movies portray the psych ward to be so scary anyway? Sure, it's been difficult and a little uncomfortable. But the few people I've interacted with here are just like me. We all have our "stuff." Maybe more people would be willing to seek help if they knew it wasn't so scary.*

A few days later, I was home and felt really good about being reunited with my family. I felt a small victory rising within myself.

I'm grateful for that experience. I was meant to be in that particular hospital at that particular time. I was meant to read that passage in a random book. I was meant to learn from strangers who are in the same place as me. I was meant to learn a valuable lesson in why it is important that I'm here on this earth and that I have purpose in life. I want to show my kids that I can be a great mom.

I have a long way to go, but I just need to have faith, hold on, trust the fact that I do indeed have purpose in this life, and keep searching for how I can be the best version of myself. I can't succumb to my fears and insecurities.

PART TWO

A NEW DIRECTION

CHAPTER SIX

CROSSING THE THRESHOLD

———

Pennsylvania. Virginia. Pennsylvania. Maryland. Virginia.

Say that five times fast!

Then, after you mastered that tongue twister, for fun let's add another Maryland and Virginia at the end. Why?

Well, four years had gone by since I had left the hospital, and in that time frame we moved to Maryland due to Alex's Navy orders, lived there for three years, I started a new job working in logistics, and we moved back to Virginia Beach due to another military transfer.

I know I asked this before, but seriously, have you kept up with all my moves yet? I wasn't kidding when I said we moved around a lot!

At this point it was 2018, and we had just moved back into the home we owned in Virginia Beach. Since we had bought the house in 2013, we rented it out for the three years that we lived in Maryland. It should have felt like déjà vu, but it felt like the exact opposite.

I was back in the same tan-colored two-story house at the end of the cul-de-sac, but the vibe felt much different. The best way to describe how I thought about the house was that it felt unfamiliar and I felt displaced. The infrastructure was the same and the familiar layout of the house made it easy to place the couches, tables, and bookshelf back where they were before.

However, the weird tension between Alex and I made being there uncomfortable because we just weren't clicking anymore. We both felt it, but we shrugged it off and tried to make sense of our new normal once again. The longer time went on, I felt depression slowly seeping in. I just wanted to go back to Maryland where my friends were. I didn't feel as confident because I wasn't in my active work environment.

Will Alex and I ever fix our marriage? Will things get back to normal between us? All I know is that it will be easy to get back into an anxious state of mind if I allow myself to, so I have to work hard to make sure that I keep those negative thoughts at bay.

I started to brainstorm. What used to bring me happiness before? Ah yes, music. I asked Alex if I could buy a digital piano because I genuinely enjoyed playing it when I was younger. As I sat down at the bench, I grazed my fingers up and down the keys of the piano while I placed my right foot on the pedal, feeling the familiarity of a time when my confidence was high due to my musical talent. Alex and the kids were watching me intently.

Without a doubt, the kids are hoping to hear me play something like Linus and Lucy from "A Charlie Brown Christmas" and Alex is hoping that his spontaneous investment proves to be worthwhile. No pressure, right?

Hoping muscle memory would kick in after all those years, I attempted to play *Pachelbel's Canon in D* and screwed it up miserably.

"Wait! Let me try again," I said as I looked at them and smiled nervously. I just kept trying, and each time I played it started to actually sound more like *Pachelbel's Canon* instead of the score from a horror film. As my confidence grew in playing the piano, I was starting to feel my self-esteem increase a tiny bit.

After eating dinner one evening, I decided to approach Alex with an idea. "So, I've been thinking..."

"What's up?" he asked, his eyes still intent on his Twitter feed as he was scrolling through his phone.

"I want to learn how to play the guitar."

"Go for it. Is there anything you can't play?" he asked, still scrolling through his phone.

Well, that was easy.

The guitar was always on my bucket list of instruments to learn, so I decided to start taking lessons at a local music store. My son, Dylan, had started learning how to play the saxophone the year before. He loved playing it and his natural musical talent had grown quickly. I don't mean to brag but yeah, he totally got it from me. He really wanted to keep improving so I signed us both up for lessons on the same night.

We decided to make Tuesday nights a tradition for us to hang out together by going to eat at Panera Bread before our lessons. I saw it as a mother/son "date night" and I loved being able to spend the one-on-one time with him. Although, if I mentioned it in the context of a mother/son date in front of him, he would adamantly deny that was what it was. God forbid! He was twelve after all.

I made myself comfortable in my chair in the tiny 10' x 10' lesson room. I set my lesson book on the music stand in front of me.

"Do you sing?"

As I tuned my rich brown-colored Ibanez acoustic guitar, I looked up at Berkley, my guitar teacher who was a bass player in his late sixties and laughed. "Now that's funny!" I replied.

He wasn't laughing. I shifted in my seat. "Oh, you're serious. Um, well, I mean I like to sing, but I don't think anyone else likes to hear me sing."

"Well, if there's one thing that will make learning the guitar easier and more fun, it's to sing as you learn. What about songwriting?"

"Um, no, I've never even thought about writing a song."

"Give it a try."

I gave him a blank stare. "Now? You want me to make up a song and sing, like, right now?"

"Yeah, show me what you got."

"While I play? Sing, out loud? While I play? What do I sing about?"

"Just pick the first thing that comes to mind. It doesn't have to rhyme or be perfect. Just sing."

Nervously, I picked up the guitar and placed my left fingers onto the neck in the C chord formation. I knew he was going to laugh at me or something.

Would anyone out in the music store hear me? I cannot have that happen. Ugh.

I strummed the chord about twenty times while clearing my throat and smiling nervously. I was put on the spot and I had to figure out what to sing that started off with this C chord that I'm playing. Out of nervousness, my vision became fixated on a purple guitar pick that was sitting on the music stand in front of me.

I started to sing very softly. "I see a guitar pick." I shook my head. *Why did I say that? Seriously? Idiot. Nerves. I blame my nerves.*

Berkley cut me off and cupped his hand around his ear. "Huh? I can't hear you."

Geez. Okay. I nervously continued, singing with a shaky voice while strumming a little louder. "Shiny purply purple guitar pick sitting right there on the music stand." Nervously, I stopped playing and said, "Well, I shouldn't have said purple twice. That was dumb. I have no clue what I'm doing. Seriously, can't I just sing a song that was already written?"

He shook his head and cut me off once again. "It's good. Louder though. Don't worry about the lyrics. Keep going and stop being nervous. It's just you and me in here. Just let go."

Oh God. I took a deep breath, found the G chord, and closed my eyes. I decided to just let my voice go loud and free. As I sang, my words came out faster and faster, and I strummed harder and harder like I was in a race against time. "Shiny purply purple shimmery gonna make me play so much better wonderfully shiny purply purple guitar pick!"

Note to self. Song writing is NOT your forte.

I heard Berkley clapping. I opened my eyes and he was actually smiling. "Great job! See? It's not that hard."

"That was the most ridiculous song ever."

"But it's your ridiculous song. I've never in my life heard a song about a purple guitar pick. That's what makes it fun!" He smiled at me.

I smiled along with him. It actually felt really good to break that comfort zone. I could have told Berkley no, I didn't want to sing. I could have succumbed to my fear of wondering what people would think about me. *After all, me, a singer? There's no way!* But after singing one verse, and thanks to his gentle nudging, I broke that barrier within myself and I finally felt empowered, confident, and successful. Maybe, just maybe, that little push out of my comfort zone and feeling good about the result was what I needed at that moment.

My confidence grew very slowly but surely. Over time, I found myself playing the guitar and singing louder and prouder even though my children and dogs were my only audience (and most of the time the kids weren't paying attention anyway). Jax and Molly, our wild and spunky Jack Russell Terriers and Ricky, our elderly Yorkshire Terrier, proved to be my consistent supporters and I was sure they had the words to The Animals' "House of the Rising Sun" and John Denver's "Take Me Home, Country Roads" drilled into their little brains. Sometimes while I was playing, I found myself thinking a lot about the change that took place within me because I didn't give in to my fear to stay comfortable.

On a warm spring day in the middle of May, I decided to take a walk during my lunch break around the lake that was just outside of my office building. It was about a 1.5-mile walk on a small thin trail that weaved in and out of trees. Turtles were sunbathing on fallen limbs protruding out of the water. Geese and their goslings were lining the trail and the surrounding grass up ahead of me. The parents were territorial, so I decided to walk off the trail out into the grass to avoid pissing off the geese and being chased.

I figured the one day that a goose would decide to chase me while jabbing my calves with its beak would be the day that everyone would be watching out their office building windows.

I can see it now: they will take videos, which will go viral, memes will be made, and I'll be the laughingstock of Virginia Beach. Fuck that! I'm not taking that chance.

As I was walking along, there was a large tree branch up ahead on the trail that had obviously been knocked down during a storm. I saw the debris blocking the trail and suddenly images from the devastation that I saw in the photos after Hurricane Maria hit Puerto Rico flashed into my mind. The Category 4 hurricane struck the island nearly eight months prior.

My heart ached knowing the death toll and from seeing the pictures of destroyed homes and buildings, fallen trees and power lines, immense flooding, and piles of trash and debris. Destruction. My grandmother was born and raised in Gurabo, Puerto Rico and I take pride in the Puerto Rican blood that flows through my veins. As I approached the tree branch and took a step over it, a crazy idea came to mind.

I wonder if they still need volunteers to help with disaster response.

I have several extended family members that still live on the island. While I knew that they were safe and that their properties didn't sustain much damage, I also knew that there were so many more people there that needed help somehow. I had given monetary donations to Hurricane Maria relief back when the storm originally hit, but I always felt guilty in the way that I wished I could have given more somehow. I had always wanted to go to Puerto Rico and learn more about my heritage culture. Perhaps going there to volunteer was the best way to approach it?

I rushed back to my desk. I pulled up Google and searched "Volunteer in Puerto Rico Hurricane Maria." The first website I saw was for a nonprofit organization called All Hands and Hearts. I clicked on the website and saw that they had an active program still going on in Puerto Rico. The type of work included concrete roof repair, debris removal, muck and gut, and mold sanitation, to name a few. *Wow.*

"I have no freaking clue how to do any of this," I said out loud. I barely even knew how to use a power drill. I didn't want to do it by myself but at the same time, I didn't even know of anyone that would go with me to do something like that. Yet, for some reason, wide-eyed and nervous, I clicked the link to apply to the program and selected May 28 as my arrival date; a date that was only two weeks away. I had no idea how it was going to pan out.

I better pick a date close in time because maybe they wouldn't need volunteers, and I would be able to say "hey, I tried' and move on with my life. I mean, can I really do this? What if they do approve me, what then? Do I try to find someone else to go with me? Do I go alone? This is way out of my comfort zone.

Wait. My comfort zone. Staying in my comfort zone and giving into my fears has created a hesitancy that has kept me from even going near the threshold of it. The concept of traveling to do this alone is terrifying to me. But, then again, so was singing in front of Berkley and look what happened when I took the risk to sing even though I was so scared to do it. I gained confidence and I was proud of myself. If I do this, if I cross this threshold and travel alone to volunteer and succeed at it, that's going to be pretty fucking awesome.

I quickly filled out the rest of the application and selected "Submit."

Within two days, there was an e-mail in my inbox from All Hands and Hearts. I was approved and invited to attend.

"Holy shit!" I said out loud, my jaw dropping to the floor. I pulled my hands up to my face and looked at my computer screen in complete shock. "Oh my God, I'm actually doing this. I'm going to Puerto Rico!" I was in disbelief.

Is this really happening? Will I know how to use the power tools? It feels so good to know that I'm going to help people there.

The next step was to get approval from Alex to go. It was hard to predict the Navy's schedule and I needed him to be home to take care of the kids while I was gone.

I never told him that I filled out the application to apply to volunteer, so this was certainly going to take him by surprise. Excited and incredibly nervous, I picked up the phone.

"Hey, um, I have a random question, and you're going to think I'm crazy."

Being prone to random questions from me, he didn't even flinch. "What's up? I'm about to go into a meeting. I have like five minutes."

"Can I go to Puerto Rico in two weeks?"

"To where?"

"Puerto Rico."

"Huh?"

"Puerto Rico?" I asked with a slight questioning tone to my voice.

"With who?"

"I'm going by myself, to volunteer for Hurricane Maria disaster response."

"Excuse me, what?"

"I'm going to volunteer…"

"I heard you, wait, where did this all come from? What are the dates?"

"I just, had an urge. I don't know. Anyway, I applied and got approved. I'm supposed to leave on Memorial Day but if you don't want me to go, I won't go."

"I got the kids. Go! It'll be good for you. But hey, I gotta run into this meeting. We'll talk more later."

Well, that went surprisingly easier than I thought. "Ahhh, I guess I'm doing this!" I squealed out loud, not sure if I wanted to feel scared or happy or what. I had never traveled alone before. I was shy and had always needed someone with me. *Can I really do this? Am I really going to be able to do construction work? What do I even pack in my suitcase for a trip like this?*

Before I could even talk myself out of it, I quickly purchased my plane ticket. *There's no backing out now. I officially have less than two weeks to mentally prepare myself for something very intimidating and on a level of something I have never done before. Alone!* Through all the nervousness, I had an underlying feeling that was telling me that this was going to be good for me. I didn't understand why at the time, but I felt somewhat proud of myself right then. I was determined to stick with that feeling.

...

Two weeks later, it was Memorial Day. I sat and watched the clock go by slowly at gate A4 at Norfolk International Airport while waiting to board my flight.

I woke up with a sense of calmness and peace that morning. I guess I was containing excitement because I didn't fully know what to expect. I hoped and prayed that the experience would help me improve myself somehow, but I didn't know exactly how that would happen or what that would look like. I was worried that I would become overwhelmed by the feeling of not being able to help enough since I could only stay for one week because of my work schedule. I hoped it wouldn't mess with my head too much.

I was excited to see what disaster response work I would be doing because I had never done any type of construction work. *I know this week is going to push me physically, mentally, and emotionally, and I have never been more ready to see how this will change my life. I have faith that it will help me somehow. In a way, just taking this first step to travel alone has me feeling accomplished already and I haven't even gotten on the plane yet.*

After a two-hour layover in Philadelphia, a four-hour flight to San Juan, and about an hour and a half drive along the thin winding roads through the mountains, I arrived safely in Barranquitas at the All Hands and Hearts volunteer base. I was still feeling nervous but so unbelievably happy at the same time. The base was set up on the grounds of a camp that a church was graciously allowing us to use and had two dormitories, a kitchen and dining hall, tool sheds, and a pavilion. In the dormitory, there were bunk beds everywhere and due to it being a coed communal living situation, there were men and women's clothing and belongings scattered throughout.

Fortunately, I was assigned a bottom bunk next to a window that already had a mosquito net in place. It was placed haphazardly, but I figured it would have to do. There wasn't any air conditioning and it was quite hot and stuffy in there. I found refuge in that window and prayed that there would be a cool breeze at night. Nonetheless, it was going to be my safe place where I would rest my head at night for the next week after working hard to help people recover from the hurricane. I pulled out my pillow, twin-size fitted bed sheet, and a light blanket that I brought with me and made my bed. I stepped back and looked at my little nook with my suitcase and backpack sitting beneath it. My little home away from home completed with an oddly placed mosquito net.

It was absolutely perfect.

After I got my bunk set up, I walked to the pavilion for the meeting. Every evening, the volunteers gathered to talk about what was accomplished during the day, the plan for the next day, and welcomed and/or said goodbye to any incoming and/or outgoing volunteers. I saw my name listed under the heading "Concrete Roof Repair" and immediately felt hesitant.

How the hell am I, of all people, supposed to help fix a concrete roof?

Better yet, since I was a new volunteer, I got to stand up in front of everyone and give my welcome speech! I am NOT a public speaker and I don't like being the center of attention. That was definitely out of my comfort zone. The eyes of about thirty volunteers were all staring at me and it felt like my surroundings went dark and a spotlight was shining down on me. They had no choice but to look at me and intently wait to hear what I had to say.

Fuck.

"Hi, um, I'm Tiffany. I'm um, from Virginia Beach in the United States. I'm, um, well, this is my first All Hands and Hearts project and I'll be here for one week. And I've never done anything like this before, so, um, I'm just going to give it my best try. Um, thank you."

Could I have been any more awkward? Did I really just say "Virginia Beach in the United States?" I could have worded that so much better. Shit.

I gave a little lazy wave as I walked back to my seat and I started to hear clapping. I looked up, and everyone was actually clapping. But it wasn't just clapping that everyone does because they had to do it. They were actually genuinely cheering, saying things like "that's awesome! Glad you are here! We're glad you came! You're going to kill it at concrete roof repair!" They were all so very warm and inviting. I felt very welcomed and immediately at ease.

After the meeting, I walked up a rocky path toward the top of a hill. I was sitting at the top of this mountain, overlooking Barranquitas. The terrain was lush and green, and the trees pronounced the individual mountain peaks. There were small colorful houses scattered throughout the mountainside. The sun was starting to set, turning the sky into a sea of pink, purple, orange, and red. The view was breathtaking, and it was absolutely gorgeous. I thought back to that moment in my office when I looked at the website and felt pure fear for even thinking about going to Puerto Rico.

I felt so proud of myself for choosing to be brave, for trusting my intuition, for booking the flight, and for not giving in to the fear of uncertainty. I knew deep down that I made the right decision.

CHAPTER SEVEN

¡PUERTO RICO SE LEVANTA!

———

Adrenaline + humidity + a failing mosquito net = sleep that wasn't worth shit.

My mosquito net, put up incorrectly before I got there, kept falling down and landing on my face and body which felt very smothering. I think I got maybe two hours of broken sleep and woke up to the sound of roosters crowing nearby. A light rain tapped on the roof and the ground outside, creating a slight coolness in the air.

After breakfast, my team lead Pete, Claudia, Bree, and I arrived at a small, square, yellow house with green bars on the windows. The house sat atop a steep large hill that overlooked some of Barranquitas. We saw the homeowner, a man in his mid-fifties, sitting on his front porch smoking a cigarette without a shirt on. A little black dog was wagging its tail at us while panting in excitement. Despite my lack of sleep, I felt a source of adrenaline, and the determination to learn replaced my nervousness about doing concrete roof repair.

"Buenos dias! Me llamo Tiffany," I said to him with a smile, extending my hand.

He shook my hand and said something very rapidly to me in Spanish.

Shit. I had no clue what he said but I didn't want to be rude. That's what I get for trying to seem confident in the little bit of Spanish that I know. Spanish is so much easier for me to read and write versus listening and replying. I looked at him with what I considered to be a smile but, since my facial expressions often show exactly what I'm feeling, my expression must have been one of confusion.

He shook his head and smiled. "I'm Israel and I do speak some English. And this," he said, picking up his little black Yorkie, "is Taquito."

"It's very nice to meet you and little Taquito," I said as I petted the soft fur on top of Taquito's head.

I gathered my yellow hard hat, safety glasses, black and pink work gloves, and my purple water bottle. I placed my hard hat on my head and it immediately slid down the right side of my head. I propped it back up, tightened the back of the strap, and it fell down to the left.

Is this seriously happening right now? Seriously, this stuff only happens to me.

I pretty much tried on all the hard hats that were available for us volunteers to use and that one was the smallest I could find. It was still too big. I swore I was the only one there who had issues with the hard hat fitting correctly.

Don't they make child-size-but-appropriate-for-an-adult models of hard hats for individuals like me who have small heads?

I pulled my baseball cap out of my backpack and placed that on my head first, then put my hard hat on top. It finally stopped shifting. I pulled out my cell phone, put it into self-ie-mode, and took a look.

"Ugh, I look absolutely ridiculous," I whispered to myself as I tried to make the hard hat/baseball hat combo look somewhat flattering. But hey, at least I was going to be safe. That's all that mattered.

I climbed up the ladder and stepped onto the roof. There were four patches of dark concrete (evidence of where the prior holes in the roof were), but they were patched up right before my arrival. The hurricane took a heavy toll on this poor man's house. Although Israel's house was located up on a hill, there was an even higher hill above him. Floodwaters rushed down over the taller hill where Israel's house was directly in the path, causing debris to pierce through his roof as well as approximately three feet of flooding inside of his house.

I honestly can't even imagine how scary that must have been. What would I have done if I saw the floodwaters rushing down the mountainside toward my house, enveloping it and filling it up with dirty, muddy, debris-filled water while I sat there helplessly? I would have been absolutely terrified.

I lifted my eyes from the concrete and was immediately mesmerized by the view. The vast landscape of Barranquitas was so pronounced from up there on the roof. There were many houses scattered about, coloring the dark green and brown mountainside with bright shades of white, pink, red, yellow, blue, orange, and bright green. There were a lot of clouds that morning, creating the image of dancing shadows on the mountains.

As beautiful as it was up there, something else caught my eye that was heartbreaking to see. Scattered all throughout the town, many houses still had blue tarps on their roofs. Seeing the amount of homes still damaged from a storm that hit eight months before was saddening. There were so many people that needed help, yet only so many volunteers to do the work.

I was suddenly overcome with worry about the fast approaching hurricane season.

What if all those roofs don't get repaired in time and another hurricane hits? What happens then? Are they going to be safe from the storm? Do the homeowners have anywhere else they can go just in case their current roof collapses?

Pete broke my train of thought by yelling at me from the ground below. "Hey, Tiffany? Do you mind grabbing this stuff for me?" He handed me two large contractor brooms and three paint rollers on extensions poles.

"Sure thing," I said, ready to take on the process of completing the roof repair.

"Here, take this bucket of primer and place it over there," he told me as he pointed to the far left corner of the roof. "Let's start by sweeping off the debris and then we'll lay down the primer."

I swept the branches, dirt, and leaves off the roof and then helped lay down some primer with one of the paint rollers. I applied the primer to the roof, ensuring the surface was coated solidly and evenly. After the primer was laid and dried properly, the next step was to apply the roof sealant.

It was time for a water break. Thank God, because I couldn't stay hydrated enough. The roof did not provide any shade from the blazing hot sun and I found that I couldn't quench my thirst enough. As I climbed down the ladder and rounded the corner onto the front porch, Israel stood and leaned against the railing, cigarette in hand.

"Were you without power for a long time after the hurricane hit?" Bree asked Israel.

"Yes, we lost power for seven months."

"Seven months?" I asked, purely in shock.

"Yes, seven months."

"How did you preserve your food that you would normally keep cold?" Pete asked.

Israel sighed. "Well, every morning I had to walk down to the general store and wait over an hour in line just for some ice and some water."

Holy shit. "You had to wait over an hour?" I asked in disbelief.

"Sometimes it would be up to three hours of waiting because the delivery trucks had a hard time getting here because of the roads being blocked."

"Wow. Man, that had to have been rough," Pete said.

Israel took a long drag of his cigarette. "It really was."

I took a drink of water and put on my sunglasses to avoid letting people see my tears. I couldn't even begin to imagine how hard that must have been. Here I thought I was inconvenienced when my power would go out for a few hours after a thunderstorm back home. Israel and so many others in Puerto Rico went literally months without power. I knew for sure that I'd never take electricity for granted again.

After a few hours of work, we drove back to the volunteer base for lunch. After being in the hot sun all morning, I was starving. Eating a warm ham and cheese sandwich with flies swarming everywhere would be a turn off for some, but I was enjoying and embracing every second. I felt gross, sticky, and sweaty, but it didn't matter. Seeing Israel come out of the house and sit there on the porch put everything into perspective. He spent seven months of his life without any power and with a leaking roof. I was so grateful that I could be there to help repair his roof so that he could live more comfortably.

The next morning, we arrived back at Israel's house and Taquito got all excited to come out and greet us. Without fail, Israel was sitting on the porch, cigarette in hand. It almost seemed like it would be weird if he didn't have a cigarette in his hand. Pete, Claudia, Bree, and I gathered our PPE (personal protective equipment) and climbed up the ladder to the top of the roof. The task of the morning was to power wash it which was something that I had never attempted before.

Having the upper arm strength of a kitten, I tried to show confidence, but the power washer was controlling me more than I was controlling it. And, of course, everyone was watching me struggle with this thing. When I pulled the trigger, the water started to spray in the opposite direction than I wanted it to because the power of the water was pushing my arm back. As I slowly started to gain control of the power washer, I started to feel the satisfaction of seeing the dirt fly away from the roof.

Power washing is actually kind of fun!

The wind happened to pick up at exactly the right time because the sun was already scorching hot and it wasn't even mid-morning yet. The wind pushed the water backward and we laughed as it sprayed us. The cold water felt so refreshing. I never imagined that I would enjoy this bonding time with complete strangers over a power washer on top of a concrete roof in Puerto Rico. We were all there together for the same reason. It was beautiful to see how people from different walks of life came together to help someone else.

When the workday was done, I walked back into the dorm. I was shocked to see that it was empty in there. I pulled out my phone and saw that it was only 3:47 p.m. We arrived back to base a little early, so the other volunteers hadn't arrived back from their worksites yet. I felt disgusting and gross and drenched in sweat.

THANK GOD I don't have to wait in line to shower.

I gathered my toiletry bag, towel, and a fresh change of clothes. The peace and quiet was such a relief and I enjoyed being alone for a few minutes. I walked toward the showers, rounded the corner, and froze.

"Oh shit!" I jumped backward. "Oh, fuck no! Oh no, fuck that!"

I lied. I wasn't completely alone. Standing between me and the middle shower stall, which had the best water pressure out of the three stalls in there, was a giant cockroach. I swore this thing was at least six inches long and was just staring me down, daring me to cross its path.

I was exaggerating; I knew it wasn't six inches long. But it sure as hell seemed like it was, with his large shell and prickly legs and mile-long antennas that were moving all around. No doubt he sensed my fear and was calling all its other cockroach friends to come torment me.

"Ugh, no. No. Ewww. Why? Why are you here? Dammit." Yes, I was whining. To a cockroach. I just didn't do creepy crawlies, especially cockroaches. I couldn't do the whole step-on-it-and-hear-it-crunch thing. That crunchy sound was so disgusting and made me want to puke.

"Can you, like, go over there?" I pleaded with the cockroach like an idiot as I pointed toward a toilet. It didn't work, obviously. The other volunteers were going to be back soon.

Suck it up, Tiffany. Just get into the freaking shower.

I cautiously took a step toward the roach and it scurried into one of the restroom stalls. I quickly hopped into the shower and hung my towel and clean clothes over the curtain rod. I peeled off the smelly and sweaty clothes that clung to my body. I turned the water on and it was freezing cold. We didn't have any hot water there but after a long productive day of working on the roof in the blistering sun, the ice-cold shower was quite a nice reward.

By 9:00 p.m., I was back in my bed, covered in bug spray, yet again thankful for the gift of having another day there. I really missed my kids but at the same time, the confidence that I was gaining from the experience was giving me a new outlook on life. I felt so motivated and it felt so good to have a sense of hope and adventure. I felt a transformation starting within me. I couldn't quite put my finger on it at the time but all I knew is that I just felt so happy.

My surroundings were unfamiliar because I wasn't used to that type of atmosphere with communal living and physical labor, but at the same time, that unfamiliarity was so new, exciting, exhilarating, and downright empowering. I smiled as I turned my head over on my pillow to face the window, welcomed the fresh mountain air, and quickly fell asleep.

...

Let's fast forward to the next afternoon. We were on a water break after laying the second coat of sealant on Israel's roof. I noticed that the muscles in my legs and lower back were getting sore, but they were welcomed pains because they reminded me that I was doing something useful, not only for my body, but for my mind as well. I also realized that I needed to put more effort into exercise so I wouldn't be as sore at the next volunteer project.

I say that with confidence–there WILL be a next time.

I didn't know when or where, but I knew it definitely would happen because the volunteering was filling that void of darkness I had in place of happiness.

I needed to use the restroom, so I stepped inside of Israel's house for the first time. The front door led right into a dining room. The bathroom was straight ahead, and then to the left was a small kitchen and a bedroom. Israel was laying on the bed with Taquito right by his feet, looking comfortable and content watching TV in the dark bedroom with the curtains drawn. There was no formal living room.

The house was small and simple, and there was something so freeing about that. I reflected on all those times I thought a change in my location or buying myself something new would make me feel better, but that never truly fulfilled me. They were only temporary fixes. I quickly discovered that what really matters is making a difference, changing lives, and helping others; that is what makes you feel rich and successful.

Maybe this was the solution that I had been searching for. That realization of what truly matters in life had brought me a sense of fulfillment and purpose, which were the pieces I had felt were missing for so long. Israel had a simple life, with a gorgeous view of the mountains of Barranquitas, and little Taquito. I learned a lot from this wonderful man, and he doesn't even know it.

...

Day four. Our team was down to three that day; it was just me, Bree, and Pete.

After applying one last final coat of sealant, we officially finished fixing Israel's roof!

I accidentally spilled some of the roof sealant on my brown steel toe boots. But as I looked at it, I smiled. It looked like a big white streak across the dark boot, almost like a lightning bolt.

Now that looks pretty freaking cool. This is going to be a forever reminder of my time in Puerto Rico whenever I wear these boots.

Before I descended from the roof, I took one last look at the mountains and the completed roof. I felt overwhelmed with joy and began crying tears of happiness.

I can't believe I actually helped complete this!

Israel could sleep peacefully at night knowing his roof wouldn't leak anymore if it rained. He would be protected if another hurricane were to hit the island.

"Señor Israel, we are all done with your roof!" Pete told him as we all lined up.

"Oh, yes, thank you so much!" Israel replied.

Bree walked up and shook his hand. "Thank you," Israel told her, nodding his head. "You're welcome! We are glad to help," Bree replied.

As Bree walked off the porch, Taquito ran over and jumped up on my leg as I approached Israel. I reached my hand out to shake Israel's hand and his eyes met mine. As he took my hand in his, I said, "Thank you for your hospitality," and smiled at him.

Tears filled his eyes, and he whispered, "Thank you. Thank you so much." My eyes started to fill up along with his and a few tears fell down my cheeks. As he held my hand and looked into my eyes, I could sense his pure gratitude. It was absolutely beautiful.

This moment right here is the exact reason why I worked so hard all week. I will never forget this moment for the rest of my life.

I inhaled more roof sealant that week than, well, ever before. Luckily, I only got a tiny bit loopy from the fumes. Those feelings of accomplishment were impactful and uplifting because I hadn't felt that confident in so long.

I was purely exhausted. My feet hurt because I wasn't used to wearing steel toe boots all day. I felt so hot. I was thirsty despite constantly drinking warm tap water. However, as I sat on the ground with my back against the side of the tool shed, dripping in sweat, I couldn't have been more grateful for the opportunity to volunteer.

That whole experience changed me. The physical work along with the gratitude in Israel's eyes made pushing myself out of my comfort zone completely worth it. I may have been far from the comforts of home, but that was exactly what I needed.

...

As I sat in the middle seat heading toward home on my flight from San Juan to Charlotte, I looked back at how much that week taught me and also how it changed me for the better.

I learned so much about perspective. Life is what we make of it. If we choose to focus on the good instead of the bad, it can make us see things in a different light.

It was miserably hot, but my focus on the work kept me strong. At times, I was tired from lack of sleep, but knowing I was helping someone gave me the adrenaline I needed to conquer each day. I may not have helped a lot of people, but I made a difference in one man's life. I wanted to take this lesson home with me and focus on the good things that were going on around me versus focusing on the things that triggered my anxiety or fear of abandonment.

Before I left for Puerto Rico, I was so excited yet also nervous about feeling incapable of doing the work I signed up to do. Now, I know I am capable of achieving anything. I gained a sense of confidence in myself that I hadn't felt in a long time. I am glad that I took that trip alone so I could really learn about myself. I was so relieved that I didn't let the words "concrete roof repair" and "mold sanitation" deter me when I originally read the description of the work.

As I think back to who I was nearly four years ago, a woman who had no hope and was on the verge of suicide, I can't help but be proud of how great it feels to be alive right now.

I have a bright future ahead and it all stemmed from traveling alone, trying something new, and helping others. I can't wait to see what happens next!

Thank you to my beautiful heritage island, Puerto Rico, for making me a better person.

Israel's concrete roof repair is complete!

CHAPTER EIGHT

AN ACTOR AND
A DIRECTOR

———

As I stared with desire, I licked my lips and my mouth watered. I craved the taste that I had been deprived of for far too long.

Ah, how the tequila, lime, and salt beckoned me. Yes, I'm talking about a margarita. You thought this chapter was going in a different direction there for a minute, didn't you? C'mon now, there's so much more of the story to tell! We have to stay on track!

We've made it to September 2018. Time flies when we are working on self-discovery, doesn't it?

Let's continue on about the margarita. I'll set the scene for you.

Summer was still very present in Virginia Beach as the temperatures were reaching the high eighties. I had plans with one of my best friends, Jessie, for drinks at Hot Tuna, a restaurant well known for its fresh and local in-season cuisine. Jessie and I have known each other for about eight years, having met when my family moved from Maryland to Virginia Beach into their cul-de-sac. She never fails to make me laugh and is also very straight up and honest about how she thinks and feels about things. Our mutual love for live music, floating on rafts in the pool, and meeting up for margaritas at happy hour are just some of the things that added to the fun of our friendship.

Jessie and I hugged and took our seats at the bar. We were in between the lunch and dinner crowd. There were open seats on either side of us creating a sense of privacy–not that we needed it, but it was nice to have. We hadn't seen each other in a couple of weeks, and we were long overdue for some girl talk. We ordered some margaritas, chips and salsa, and calamari.

We took sips of our margaritas. Mine had extra salt on the rim, just as I love it. Not being one to drink very often, a few sips already had me feeling happier and a tiny bit buzzed.

What I admire most about Jessie is her genuine loving and beautiful heart. She is one of the co-founders of a local Virginia Beach-based nonprofit organization called AIDNOW which helps the at-risk and homeless youth in kindergarten through twelfth grade. Every August, they hold an event called Jump Start, which is an event where the children receive clothes, shoes, backpacks, school supplies, food, hygiene products, books, haircuts, and medical, dental, and vision screenings. It is a way for the kids to get a "jump start" on their school year.

I volunteered at this event five times and have always loved helping the children pick out their new clothes. Seeing how something as simple as a new shirt or new pair of shoes can make a child smile is a very heartwarming experience.

"Oh my God! I have SO much to catch you up on!" I said to Jessie excitedly.

The next twenty minutes consisted of me talking to her about everything in life from stuff the kids were up to, funny stories and frustrations that were happening in my marriage, the upcoming Avett Brothers concert that I had tickets to, my thoughts on the color and style I might get at my upcoming hair appointment.

Her expression from the beginning of the conversation had changed from a smile to a blank stare with slow blinking. She finished her margarita and had already ordered another one. Mine was still almost full and she kept looking over at it, hoping I would get the hint to start drinking it.

I was still rambling, as that's usually what happens when the tequila kicks in. "Oh and wait until you hear about this! The other day I–"

She cut me off mid-sentence. "Will you drink your margarita already?"

We both laughed hysterically. God, I love her. Her no-nonsense-I'm-not-afraid-to-tell-you-how-it-is attitude makes her fiery and fierce.

"Oh geez, have I really been talking that much?"

She looked at me with one eyebrow raised and a facial expression that said, "You have got to be kidding me." No words were needed.

"Okay, your turn. I'll shut up and drink my margarita," I said as I smiled and took a sip out of my straw.

"So, I have a question for you," Jessie said with an excited smile on her face.

"Okay," I replied in a curious tone because I never know what Jessie's mind is up to. We literally talk about anything and everything.

"So, something I've always wanted to do with AIDNOW is take it internationally, focusing on helping in education, like we do here. You studied anthropology and your trip to Puerto Rico was inspiring. We've already discussed this as a board, but how would you like to join the board and help us branch out internationally?"

"Wait, what? You want me to do international projects for AIDNOW?" I asked excitedly.

"Yes," she responded, laughing at me because I must have had a crazy look on my face that was a combination of shock and excitement.

"Oh my God, yes of course! I'd be honored!" I answered right away.

Is this really happening? This is such a dream come true for me. I feel like the anthropology and volunteer work integration that I was so desperately seeking is finally coming to fruition. Who would have thought that it would have been with AIDNOW, the non-profit I enjoy volunteering with so much? Oh wow, there's so much to consider. I was automatically thinking of things on a grand scale. *What kind of work will we be doing? Where will we be traveling to?*

"What are you guys thinking you want to do? Do you have a plan?" I asked, already wanting to take on my new role right there at the bar.

"Well, since my family has Mexican roots, I was thinking of doing a project somewhere in Mexico. Look, it's your show and you will be directing it. Do some research and planning, and then present it to us at a future board meeting. But yeah, this is going to be exciting!"

Ah, Mexico. I couldn't be more excited about returning back to Mexico. In January 2017 and 2018, Alex and I went to see the Avett Brothers "At the Beach," which were four-day music festivals in Riviera Maya, Mexico.

Yes, I love the Avett Brothers so much that I traveled all the way to Mexico twice to see them. They really are THAT good!

During our time there, I volunteered with the nonprofit organizations Positive Legacy and Dreams for Mayan Children for a day during each trip in the Mayan villages of Dos Palmas and Chemuyil. I assisted in painting a school, planted fruits and vegetables, cleaned up trash, and helped build a futbol (soccer) field.

The women in the village prepared us the most amazing authentic Mayan meal consisting of chicken, rice, beans, and handmade tortillas that tasted so fresh and delicious. After lunch, the children of the village performed a song and dance for the volunteers, and the village Shaman performed a Mayan ritual involving incense to cleanse our negative energy. Being in the village reawakened my love for anthropology, which had been lying dormant within me for so long.

I was feeling really nervous about this new role with AIDNOW though. I was nervous because I am an introvert and a natural follower rather than a leader. I have a fear of public speaking, and the thought of leading and supervising is terrifying, to say the least. I think it stems from me being uncomfortable with confrontation. The discomfort with confrontation goes back to my childhood. I'm just naturally a passive person and I don't enjoy upsetting people.

If I was in a leadership position and had to fire someone, I think I would cry. Well, to be honest, I know I would cry.

What if I take on a project too big and I screw it up? What if I'm not a good leader? The board is going to place their trust in me. Am I going to screw all this up? Deep down I know it's all fear because, after all, becoming a leader is something that is way out of my comfort zone.

But then, it hit me.

I was so nervous and scared to go to Puerto Rico, but afterward, I felt empowered by the experience. *What if this is another opportunity to push myself into something I've been afraid of? What if this makes me even more confident? Maybe if I just have faith and give it a try, even though I'm scared to death of doing it, it will work out. The thought of knowing that an international project that helps to foster education as a result of my research and planning is pretty freaking awesome!*

All of a sudden, I felt a twinge of bravery and approached the situation from a mindset of positivity versus fear. Having already volunteered in the Mayan villages, I felt that a project similar to those would be a great first step. I knew exactly who to call to get this process rolling–my good friend Crystal.

I first met Crystal when volunteering in the village of Dos Palmas in Mexico in 2017. Originally from Virginia, Crystal is a single mom of two teenagers and has been living in Mexico for over twenty years. After surviving a horrific car accident that shattered her left humerus and caused multiple fractures to her right femur and hip, she was left permanently physically disabled.

Despite that obstacle, she was determined to find ways to uplift her spirits as well as take care of her children. She founded the nonprofit organization Sonrisas Contagiosas and worked with another nonprofit–Dreams for Mayan Children. Both nonprofits involve ecotourism, which is a way to bring tourists out of the all-inclusive resorts and introduce them to authentic Mayan culture by encouraging them to volunteer and help meet the needs of the indigenous people in the Mexican Yucatan Peninsula.

"Hi Crystal!"

"Oh my goddess, Tiffany! How are you? It's so good to hear from you!"

"I'm doing good! So, I have some big news!"

"Tell me. What is it?"

"Well, I just took on the role of International Missions Director for a local nonprofit organization here in Virginia Beach called AIDNOW. They want to branch out internationally and asked me to lead the project. They want to start in Mexico."

"How exciting! That's amazing!"

"I know, right? So, I automatically thought of you since we met in Dos Palmas and then I worked with you again in Chemuyil. My question is, are there any other villages that need help similar to the work we did before? Ideally, we are thinking something along the lines of working on a school again."

"Wonderful! Yes, there are! I'll get you in touch with Patty, she's the founder of Dreams for Mayan Children. I know she's been working with a village called Nuevo Durango and I know their kindergarten school could use an upgrade. Nuevo Durango is an indigenous village in the jungle and it's about a one-hour drive west of Tulum."

"Oh wow, that's awesome! Yes, I definitely want to get in touch with Patty!"

"Absolutely. This is exciting! I can't believe we are going to be working together again. This is amazing!"

"I know! I can't wait to see where thisrk leads. Thank you, Crystal!"

I need to pinch myself. This is crazy! I can't believe this is happening! Nobody is around to see the smile on my face right now, but that's okay. Some great things are going to come out of this project. I'm nervous but I'm ready for the challenge.

…

"Hey, are you busy this Saturday?"

It was a cold Tuesday morning in early November. I looked up from my desk and Tim, one of my coworkers who is a retired Navy Master Chief, was standing in the doorway.

"Not that I know of, why?"

"How would you like to volunteer to be a victim?"

At that point, I wasn't quite sure how to answer that question. We all know by now that I can't hide my facial expressions, so my puzzled look surely prompted further explanation.

"There's a CERT tornado drill this Saturday morning and they need victims. Basically, they do the whole movie makeup thing, make you up to have injuries, and then the CERT students will perform search and rescue and triage. It's like their final exam."

"Oh really?" I asked. "That's so interesting!"

"Yeah, the injuries look pretty realistic too. We have intestinal injuries where the guts are coming out, broken limbs with bones sticking out, blood, you know, all that crazy stuff."

CERT stands for Community Emergency Response Team. I had never been done up in movie makeup and, being a huge fan of Halloween, I was secretly hoping for something gory and gruesome.

"Oh, how neat! Yes, absolutely I'll go!"

A dreary gray sky was left behind from an early morning rain on the following Saturday morning. I arrived at the church at 7:30 a.m. where they were holding the tornado drill. Tim was the only person that I knew there and since he was running around helping get everything set up, I found my way to the moulage (makeup) area and sat off to the side by myself. The moulage area was set up in one of the large rooms of the church. There were two tables with all the makeup and tools set up on them. A few of the "victims" were already there, scrolling through their phones while we waited.

Marie, one of the CERT volunteers/makeup artists, addressed the group. "While we wait for the other victims to show up, feel free to grab a donut or two off the table in the back."

Well, you don't have to tell me twice.

I rushed over to the donuts and opened the box. "Beautiful," I whispered as I opened the first box. I grabbed two chocolate frosted donuts with orange, red, and green sprinkles. I mean, she did say one or two. I will always opt for two if offered.

About halfway through my second donut, Marie stood in front of the makeup tables. She had a huge smile on her face, and she looked so peppy and excited. She had way too much energy for that early in the morning.

"Okay, all of our victims are here. So, welcome everybody! Don't forget; the more real your injuries are, the better! This is their final exam, so when the injuries are realistic, it can throw them off. That's the point; we want them to be able to act under pressure and remember what they learned throughout the course. Now before we begin, does anyone have any health issues or injuries that we need to know about so that it does not get confused with your acting?"

I had just taken a bite of the donut and started to chew it very slowly with wide eyes.

Wait, what? Did I hear her right? Acting? I have to act out my injuries? How on earth am I supposed to do that? You have got to be kidding me. I don't like to be the center of attention. People will be watching me! I swallowed the bite of the donut and my stomach was in knots. *I shouldn't have taken two donuts. Dammit. Great! Now I'm anxious.*

As Marie assigned injuries to people, the seasoned veterans of the drill talked about how they were going to yell for help and scream in pain and agony. My heart started beating faster and goosebumps were covering my arms. I had never acted before, let alone acted injured in front of a group of strangers.

Marie pointed to a tall, thin, dark-haired girl in her late teens or early twenties. "Anna, okay, you are going to be pregnant with a broken leg. I have a pillow here you can use so that we can make you look pregnant. And when they come in, you are going to go into labor."

Well, that's something I can probably do. I mean, I have had three children before.

Marie pointed her pen toward me and then looked down through her list of permissible injuries to use for this drill. "Tiffany, let's see here."

Oh Lord, here we go. What am I going to have to act out? This is nerve-wracking. Pick something easy for me, Marie. Please let it be something easy.

"Okay!" she exclaimed, with enthusiasm in her voice. Barely taking a breath and talking faster and faster, she said, "You are going to have a dislocated elbow, so we are going to make it all bruised and ugly-looking. Oh! And there is going to be a piece of glass in your neck and it'll be bleeding, but as you're acting you won't know that it's bleeding because you lost your infant baby in the tornado so you're panicking!" She excitedly walked over to the table, pulled a baby doll in pink clothing out of the bag, and hurriedly walked back over to hand it to me. "Meet your baby!" she said as she laughed.

I nervously laughed back as I took the doll from her.

Is this lady serious?

I looked at the doll with apprehension; it just smiled and stared at me.

Why couldn't I be the pregnant one?

Marie walked over and gathered the supplies needed to start the makeup application.

She applied makeup to my elbow, making it look very bruised, and then applied a mold to my neck with a piece of sharp plastic sticking out of it and fake blood trickling down.

She did this all in about ten minutes and it looked pretty realistic. However, I was still nervous.

It's one thing to see the injuries on me when I look in a mirror but it's another thing to actually try to feel them and act them out. On top of that, I have to scream and yell for help? Oh, and act like I lost my baby on top of it? My pretend doll baby. I mean, no pressure. No pressure at all. Are you kidding me?

The CERT coordinators set me and my "baby" up in a preschool classroom that had no evidence of a tornado hitting it besides the six child-sized yellow chairs that were turned over onto their sides on the far right side of the classroom. All around the room were toys that were too neatly organized, and posters covering the walls with bible verses, letters, and numbers. That literally had to be the tidiest and cleanest classroom I had ever seen in my entire life.

I was told to hide the baby somewhere and when I heard voices in the hallway I had to start yelling for help. They left and shut the door. I looked around, confused, wondering how on earth I was going to pull this off.

Are they just leaving me in here? I still don't know what I'm supposed to do!

I placed the baby under one of the small tables across the room where the little chairs were knocked over. I walked across the room and assessed my surroundings. The baby wasn't camouflaged at all. Anyone could clearly see her. I placed my fingers on my temples and applied pressure.

Oh my God, this is going to be a disaster!

I sat on the rug on the floor that was designed with roads and railroad tracks made for little cars and trains. I traced my fingers around the bending roads, trying to amp up my courage. It wasn't working. Seconds turned into minutes, and minutes turned into an hour. The temperature was cold in there and I was still sitting on the floor wishing I had brought a sweater. I looked down at my bruised elbow.

Should I lay down on the floor so that when they walk in, they find me in distress? I tried to lay down and felt absolutely ridiculous. I looked at the clock on the wall–one hour and fifteen minutes had passed since I first sat on the rug. I was beginning to wonder if I was forgotten about in there.

And now I have to pee. Of course I have to pee. I mean, why wouldn't I? This is just my luck.

Out of nowhere, I heard the other volunteers start calling for help. "Help! Help me! Get me out of here! I'm hurt, please!" They were yelling, pleading loudly and fearfully, and it sounded realistic.

"Damn, they are good. Okay I got this," I said out loud to myself. I stood up, cradled my left elbow in my right hand, and opened my mouth. "Help," I said in the softest, most monotone boring voice ever. I laughed at myself. *I sound like an idiot!* I didn't know why I was so embarrassed. I just kept saying help in a very quiet voice, feeling more and more discouraged.

After what felt like an eternity, the door to the room opened. All of a sudden, a bunch of CERT volunteers entered the room wearing hard hats and green reflective vests. I don't know where it came from, but everything in the room just kind of blacked out, and I broke into character unexpectedly.

"My baby, I lost my baby! Please, you have to help me find my baby!" I yelled, pleading with them, looking frantically around the room with wide eyes and heavy breaths. I don't even know how many people were in the room with me. Although I could see the doll under the table and I knew they could see it too, I just channeled the thought of what it would feel like if I actually lost my child. That was the only thing I chose to focus on. My surroundings didn't feel real in that moment and it didn't seem like I was in the preschool room at all.

"Ma'am, it's going to be okay. We'll find your baby. Please sit down so we can assess your injuries."

"I don't care about my injuries! Where is my baby?" I yelled out. Some of the CERT volunteers were standing there, looking nervous and confused by my facial expressions and yelling.

An older gentleman got down on one knee and looked me in the eyes. "Ma'am, we'll find your baby, I promise. What's your name?"

"Tiffany," I responded, as I nervously looked around the room with tears in my eyes.

"Okay Tiffany, I'm Kevin. Do you know what day it is?"

"It's Saturday. Where's my baby? Please, my baby," I pleaded with them, pretty much hyperventilating from forcing myself to breathe heavily.

"Good. Tiffany, everything is going to be okay. I see your arm is injured and you are bleeding from the neck."

"I'm what?" They were showing true concern for my injuries and for losing my baby. It gave me ammunition to keep acting.

"Tiffany, you are going to be okay. You just have something in your neck. We have to look at the wound in your neck." He was so calm and caring. *I almost feel bad for yelling, but I feel like it's what I have to do to make this realistic.* "Can you move your arm?"

I tried to stretch it out and winced in pain. "Ouch, No! No, it hurts too bad! And I don't care about my neck! Just find my baby! You promised you were going to find my baby!" I screamed angrily.

"Ma'am, I found your baby," a young man in his early twenties said as he handed me the baby. He had her cradled in his arms like a real infant and handed her to me very carefully.

"Oh my God, thank you! Thank you so much!" I said as I held her. *Now I feel like I'm going to pass out from breathing so heavy. I give mad props to actors and actresses. This acting stuff is no joke.*

Kevin helped me up off the chair. He and the other CERT volunteers escorted me out of the room and walked me to the triage area. As soon as I rounded the corner, Tim was waiting there with an impressed look on his face, mouthing "wow!" and gave me a thumbs up. Seeing the impression on not only his face, but on several of the CERT members' faces, made me realize that I actually did a good job.

I can't believe I pulled this off. As ridiculous as it felt to act that out, it was pretty cool to see them taking my injuries and situation seriously while expressing concern for me. *It would be really cool to do this again. I wonder what I'll act out next time. I realize that once again, I pushed myself way out of my comfort zone and gained an incredible amount of confidence afterward. I feel really good about myself right now and I'm ready to take on the rest of my Saturday and make it a productive one.*

This stepping out of my comfort zone thing is starting to become a healthy trend...who would have thought?

CHAPTER NINE

A SELFLESS SIGNATURE

"Um, Mom, I have to tell you something."

It was early March 2019, and Dylan and I were heading to Panera Bread and music lessons for our unofficial don't-call-it-a mother/son Tuesday date night. The lessons were going really well, and his talent had improved tremendously. His passion for playing saxophone was steadily increasing. I was enjoying my guitar lessons with Berkley and, while I didn't make the time to practice as much as I should, I loved learning new songs and techniques. Dylan was nervous and fidgeting in the passenger seat.

"Okay, what is it?" I asked him.

"Um, well, you know how I've been thinking a lot about going to live with my dad?"

"Yeah?" I could already tell where this was going. He was uncomfortable and very hesitant.

"Well, I've been thinking, and I made the decision that I definitely want to go live with him."

Well, that felt like a knife straight into my heart. I knew this day was going to come eventually but I just wasn't expecting it to be so soon. Ever since the divorce, I made sure that Elora and Dylan had a great relationship with their dad, Joe.

Dylan and his dad are very close, and he had been wrestling for the past two years with deciding if he wanted to explore what living with him would be like.

We had multiple discussions about what that would look like, how much of a transition it would be, and how it would change the family dynamic since he wouldn't have me, Elora, or his younger brother Mason under the same roof as him anymore. Despite how heavy the topic was for me to handle, Joe and I were both fully supportive of him throughout the decision-making process.

"Okay, well, when are you thinking that you want to move out there? When you start high school or something?"

"Um, well, actually, I want to start eighth grade there."

"Eighth grade? So that means you would have to move out there this summer."

"Yeah."

I was heartbroken. I swallowed the lump that had formed in my throat and I fought back tears.

My thirteen-year-old son is going to be moving away in about four months. Is this really happening?

"Okay, well, I'll talk to your dad and we'll get the process started. Are you one hundred percent sure this is what you want?" I tried my best to sound supportive but all I really wanted to do was beg and plead with him to stay another year or two.

I'm not ready for this.

"Yeah," he said, almost shamefully, and I knew it was because he was afraid of hurting my feelings.

Dylan and I have always been close. When he was younger, he was obsessed with Thomas the Train and we would spend hours setting up tracks and playing with the trains together. He played several seasons of flag football before we moved back down here to Virginia Beach and throwing the football back and forth out in the yard was a daily activity. We enjoyed watching *The Office* together, sharing memes back and forth on Facebook or through text messages, and of course, our music lesson nights.

The sweetest thing, though, is that ever since he was little, he never liked being too far away from me. He always liked hanging out in the same room as me even if we were doing separate things.

What am I going to do when I don't have him here every day anymore? Well, I'll figure that part out later. Right now, I have to be strong for him.

"Dylan, I love you, and most of all I want you to be happy. So, if you feel that this is something that will make you happy, then I will support you in this decision."

"Okay," he said. In his voice, I could tell he was unsure whether or not to believe that I was fine with it.

I always figured I had more time, and that he would wait until he was transitioning to high school to leave. I now have to say goodbye to him sooner than I would like.

It was one of those times when I started to wonder where I went wrong as a mom.

Why doesn't he want to stay with me?

I would never ask him that question because I didn't want him to feel guilty for his decision. Inside, it tore me apart. I tried to convince myself that it was about him furthering his relationship with his dad and that it wasn't about me and my parenting. Still, no matter how much I tried to compartmentalize those thoughts, I still couldn't help but wonder if it was somehow all my fault.

He is going to be living four hours away from me though. How often will I see him? Is he going to forget about me? Will the relationship that I have with my son change? Will that beautiful bond we have fade away? Will he not need me as his mom anymore?

Joe's fiancé, Lori, is amazing and has always cared for Elora and Dylan as if they were her own. I had no doubts about his safety and well-being there, but I couldn't help but wonder if he was going to think that she is a better mom than I am. I have come so far in building my confidence and the thought of letting these abandonment triggers take me back to where I was five years before ago was so scary to me.

I can't go back to those self-destructive tendencies of isolation, living constantly in fear, or wrestling with the thoughts of whether life is worth living or not. I refuse to go back to that mindset. I have to figure out a way to make peace with this situation and focus on the positive things that can result from this.

While the onset of spring meant warmer temperatures, longer hours in the day, and colorful blooms of petals on flowers and leaves on trees, spring also meant that we as a family were about to endure yet another eight-month Navy deployment.

The months leading up to this deployment were full of tension, arguments, and talks of separation and possible divorce. There was no doubting that Alex and I were both withdrawing from each other in a way to protect ourselves from hurt individually, and to be honest I was relieved that he left because I just needed a break from the constant disagreements. We both picked each other apart; after all, it's easier to say goodbye to someone when you are angry with them. The easiest thing for me to do was to just keep to myself and protect my heart.

The night we took him to the Navy base to say our goodbyes, I had a very weird and uncomfortable feeling in the pit of my stomach; a feeling that things were going to take a turn for the worst while he was gone and that I was going to find myself a single mother again. My strength in dealing with my fears was going to be tested to the core that year.

Elora, Dylan, Mason, and I tried to adjust to the new normal of me as a full-time working single mom, graduate student, and board member for AIDNOW.

I was two courses into my Human Security and Resilience graduate program which focused on the seven aspects of human security (food, health, economic, political, environmental, community, and personal) and how people around the world in different socioeconomic situations face hardships like starvation and disease, especially in times after natural disasters, terrorist attacks, or humanitarian crises as a result of armed conflicts. I decided to go back to school because I genuinely love to learn, and I wanted to take my career in a humanitarian aid direction that involves helping others.

It felt so good to no longer feel shame for studying the subjects that I love. I got asked all the time what I was going to do with my degree when I graduated, and to be honest I had absolutely no idea. For some reason, I enjoyed the beauty of that unknown.

I am naturally a planner, a list-maker, a woman who needs to have everything lined up and figured out in order to feel comfortable with a situation. For the first time, I let go of that control and allowed myself to have faith and feel confident that opportunities would present themselves when the time was right. If I were to have made the decision to attend graduate school solely on the fact that I needed to have a plan in place after graduation, then I would have never started.

...

"If you agree with everything that has been laid out on the paperwork, then the next thing you need to do is sign on this line, and that signature will state that you are relinquishing your rights as the primary physical custodian of Dylan."

May had arrived, and I was sitting next to Joe across the desk from a court mediator. We were in a tiny office that was adjacent to a courtroom. The dark shiny mahogany desk took up most of the room and offered a stark contrast to the gray walls. I looked down at the paperwork that was in front of me. I tried to control the pen as my hand shook nervously. The tears in my eyes were clouding my vision and the words on the paperwork blurred together like large blobs of black ink that had no rhyme or reason.

I froze.

This is the moment I have been fearing for years; the moment where I selflessly sign the custody of my son over to his dad. I had tried everything I could to mentally prepare myself for this moment but now that it's here, all I can do is freeze. Maybe, if I just freeze, this whole thing will go away. Maybe this moment isn't even real. I just need more time. I'm not ready.

"Is everything okay?" the mediator asked me, with concern in her voice.

"I think everything is just hitting her all at once and reality is setting in," Joe said as he placed his hand on my back for a few seconds, trying to comfort me. I immediately started to cry.

After about thirty long seconds, I gathered myself and tried to start thinking rationally.

Shaking my head and wiping my tears, I said, "I'm sorry. Okay, I'm sorry. Um, okay, um, geez. Okay." I fumbled my words.

What if me signing this form turns out to be a bad thing? What if this is the moment that I lose the relationship that I have with my son?

Knowing deep down that this was what Dylan wanted, and out of genuinely wanting him to be happy, I hurriedly signed my name on the line and threw the pen down. I couldn't control the tears that followed. I wanted to be comfortable with it, I really did, but as a mother I couldn't help but feel that I wasn't supposed to prepare for my son to leave until after high school graduation.

Why do I have to deal with this now? He's only thirteen. He still needs me as his mom. I just signed a paper that is going to change everything. Will I ever make peace with this decision? My baby boy is leaving the nest. I can't dwell on the negative parts of this.

All I could do at that point was just try to enjoy the time I did have with him, focus on the positive things, and have faith that the experience and new chapter in his life would help him become a stronger young man.

CHAPTER TEN

PANIC! AT THE AIRPORT

———

"Would you rather explore outer space or the deep ocean?"

Ah, the million-dollar question.

It was mid-August 2019, and the dreaded volunteer welcome speech time at the Hurricane Florence disaster relief program in Bayboro, North Carolina.

I was in the middle of a course called Foundations of Resilience for my graduate program and one of the requirements involved volunteering for a nonprofit that focused on international outreach. When I found out about the project, I immediately thought of All Hands and Hearts, the organization that I volunteered with in Puerto Rico. On September 14, 2018, Category 1 Hurricane Florence made landfall near Wrightsville Beach, North Carolina, leaving immense flooding and devastation in her wake.[4]

I had already given my basic boring speech that lacked total personality: "Hi, um, I'm Tiffany and I'm from Virginia Beach. This is my second time volunteering with All Hands

———

4   "Hurricane Florence: September 14, 2018," National Weather Service, accessed August 31, 2020.

and Hearts; the first was in Barranquitas. Oh, and I'll be here for one week."

As I tried to run back to my seat to avoid being in the spotlight any longer than I needed to be, Toni, the bubbly and fun Logistics Coordinator who was wearing bright rainbow knee-high socks, threw in the question about exploring space or the ocean after I finished talking.

I was put on the spot and stood there with my mouth slightly open.

"Um..."

All eyes were on me. Everyone was dying to know what my answer was going to be.

Dammit, how do I choose between the two?

It was a serious question that required serious thought. One can't take this type of question lightly.

"Um..." I needed to hurry up though. It was almost dinnertime, after all. The smell of lasagna was distracting me.

Do I follow my childhood dream of being an astronaut and flying the space shuttle, gallivanting across different planets while identifying the possibility of the truth about aliens and other intelligent life forms? Or do I dare to defy that childhood dream and choose the vast open oceans, floating alongside the abundant sea life in my tiny submarine, discovering Atlantis, taking a selfie with a beautiful mermaid or a hunky merman, and explore countless shipwrecks while uncovering their magnificent history?

"Open ocean. No doubt."

"Awesome!" Toni said.

Besides, I was about to be single again. The thought of a muscly merman was much sexier than an alien. A girl can dream, right?

...

"Hey Tiffany, have you ever used a Sawzall before?"

Amy, my team lead, asked me that question as she held up a hand-held power tool with a small reciprocating saw blade on it. We were in the middle of mucking and gutting the drywall and insulation of a mold-infested home.

Um, excuse me? A what? I really need to brush up on my power tool knowledge.

"No, I haven't, but I'll definitely try it!"

After a quick tutorial, she handed me the tool.

The temperatures that week soared well into the nineties and the humidity was brutal. It felt good to be wearing the same purple All Hand and Hearts volunteer work shirt, concrete-covered jeans, and steel toe boots that I wore in Puerto Rico. I considered them to be my good luck charms.

I must admit, using the Sawzall to cut apart a piece of mold-infested wood felt quite therapeutic. The vibration of it also made me feel like my hands were shaking for a few minutes after I put it down. Regardless, learning about and using the power tools made me feel pretty badass and increased my confidence even more.

My first time using a Sawzall on a mold-infested cabinet in Bayboro, North Carolina.

"For those of you going to Squids tonight, the first van will be leaving in ten minutes," Tuna, our volunteer relations coordinator, announced.

Kristina, nicknamed Tuna, was like the mother hen of us volunteers. Her fun and spunky personality made me feel welcome from the moment I arrived on the volunteer base and she never failed to make everyone laugh and smile.

"What is Squids?" I asked Joe, another volunteer.

"Oh, Squidders! It's a bait and tackle shop that's close to here where we hang out, have a drink, and do karaoke and stuff twice a week."

Karaoke? And drinks? At a bait and tackle shop? Well, I have to check this out.

Squidders Supply Store was a convenience store with all the local fisherman's bait and tackle needs. In the back of the store, there were drink coolers with some options for beer. I grabbed a Redd's Apple Ale, turned around, and went back toward the register.

Russell and Debbie, the store owners, greeted me with a smile.

"Are you a new volunteer? I don't recall seeing you here yet," Russell said as I handed him a five-dollar bill.

"Yes, I am! This is quite a cute place you have here!"

"Why thank you. We like to stay open late two nights a week just for y'all to come out and have fun. We appreciate all the things you do for us down here and helping the community. It's the least we can do."

"That's amazing!"

"I even bought that TV there and set up some karaoke for y'all. I'll get it fired up in a little while!" he said as he pointed to the small TV mounted on the wall behind me.

After an hour of cornhole, Jenga, and socializing, the karaoke scene was ready to go. Russell lowered the lights and had some purple party lights glowing throughout the front of the store.

"Are you gonna sign up to sing?" John, another volunteer, asked me. Earlier in the day, I assisted John in debris removal from several of the worksites. John spent many years traveling the world volunteering in disaster response and Habitat for Humanity projects.

Oh hell no. I'm not singing. Not happening. I'm not ready for that kind of performing quite yet!

"No, not this time," I said with a hesitant laugh.

"Are you sure?"

"I'm quite positive," I replied, still laughing.

Rachel, a younger woman who also studied anthropology and was getting ready to join the Peace Corps, took the "stage," which was really just the area next to the ice cream cooler. The opening piano riff to Journey's "Don't Stop Believin'" started and other volunteers started to cheer.

I was never particularly fond of that song before. In fact, whenever I heard it on the radio I would cringe, but the experience of having Rachel sing it along with the volunteers laughing, singing, and dancing together after a day of helping people whose homes were damaged by the hurricane, changed my viewpoint of it completely.

I can't believe I'm thinking this, but this song isn't that bad. It's kind of.. catchy. This is actually really fun!

It was amazing how some volunteer work and a night out with some of the most beautiful souls in the world changed my mindset on something that I thought so negatively about before.

In case you were wondering, no, I didn't put "Don't Stop Believin'" on my Spotify playlist yet. Baby steps, people.

...

Once I returned from North Carolina, I had to switch gears and put on my board member hat to get ready for Jump Start, AIDNOW's annual back-to-school event for the homeless and at-risk students in Virginia Beach. It was my first time being at that event as a board member, and I was nervous and excited to take on a supervisory role and lead a team of volunteers.

The middle school where we held the event was set up like a store at the mall and every family got their own personal shopper to help them find the perfect back-to-school outfits. Words can't describe the feeling of seeing a child's face light up and smile because they never had a brand new pair of shoes before. It was so heartwarming.

I was helping a mother find a coat for her young son, who was probably around six or seven years old. She told me his favorite color was blue. As I looked through the coats we had available, I came across a little blue jacket that looked to be his size that had Mickey Mouse on the back. I held it up in the air, and as he saw it his eyes lit up. He smiled so big, ran up to me, and grabbed the coat, holding it so tightly. I helped him try it on and he just danced and jumped around, his smile beaming from ear to ear. He gave me a hug, and tears of joy came to my eyes.

Being able to help and serve others was in turn helping me in my recovery. I noticed that each time I volunteered and experienced the feeling of gratitude from those who I was helping, it opened my heart to feel more uplifted and free. Working alongside likeminded people and working together to support each other created a community that was full of encouragement and positivity.

...

Oh crap, did I forget to pack my bathing suit?

It was only 4:30 a.m. but it was already a hot, humid, late August Saturday morning. I was digging through my backpack that was sitting in my lap at gate A4 at Norfolk International Airport. I was heading to Nuevo Durango, a tiny indigenous Mayan village in the jungle of the Yucatan Peninsula in Mexico.

The purpose of the trip was to meet with Patty, the founder of Dreams for Mayan Children which was also the nonprofit that I was going to be working with for my International Missions Director position with AIDNOW. We were going to be figuring out a game plan for a school restoration project in the village.

The departure gate seemed quite nostalgic because it was the same gate for my volunteer trip to Puerto Rico, although the last time I was there, my morning went a lot smoother.

I was traveling alone again, and the trip made me really nervous because everything started going wrong. Since I couldn't take too much time off work, it was supposed to be a quick weekend trip with me flying down on a Friday afternoon and flying back on Sunday evening. However, my flight on Friday got cancelled at the last minute due to thunderstorms.

I also found out two days prior to my departure that a friend who was supposed to pick me up at the airport could no longer do so because of mechanical issues with his car. I had to book a rental car last minute, meaning that I had to drive by myself in Mexico.

The thought of driving alone in a foreign country was nerve-wracking and out of my comfort zone but I tried to stay positive.

I placed my backpack down onto the floor between my feet and it fell over, knocking over the fresh cup of hot tea that I had just bought at Starbucks minutes prior.

"Ugh, no, no, no!" I whispered, picking the cup up as quickly as I could before too much spilled out. In my mind, the tea was rushing out of the little drinking hole like Niagara Falls, dumping all over the ground.

I looked around quickly, praying that nobody saw a thing. Thankfully, it was so early in the morning that most of the passengers were either sleeping, scrolling through their phones, or were slumped in their chairs looking blankly straight ahead, almost like zombies trying to come to life.

Thank God I at least had a lid on the cup.

Using some napkins that I had in one of the side pockets of my backpack, I cleaned up the mess as much as I could and discretely placed my foot over the spot on the ground, hoping that nobody would notice.

I slumped back in my seat, closed my eyes, and sighed heavily. I then leaned forward, placed my elbows on my thighs and buried my head in my hands while on the verge of tears. My anxiety was starting to get the best of me.

Am I really going to be able to drive in Mexico by myself? Was yesterday's flight cancellation a sign that maybe this is all too risky? My return flight is tomorrow afternoon; is it worth traveling all the way down there for not even forty-eight hours? What was I thinking? What's the speed limit there anyway? What if I get lost or break down on the side of the road? Am I going to get kidnapped?

And where the hell is my bathing suit?

I picked up my backpack and continued to search it frantically, expecting to see the little black strings pop out from somewhere. There was a cenote (an underwater swimming hole) close to the village and I knew I would be going to swim in it at some point due to the intense heat of the jungle. Of course, the bathing suit was nowhere to be found.

I guess swimming isn't in my near future after all. This sucks.

The truth of the matter was that all the anxiety and nervousness was not just about forgetting a bathing suit or having to drive a car in Mexico. Was I nervous about that? Yes, but the emotions I felt that morning were a build-up of emotions from the past several months.

In July, I had to help Dylan pack all his belongings and he moved to live with his dad. There was an emptiness in the house as well as in my heart because I didn't have him there all the time with me anymore. Packing the trunk of the car with all his clothes, his saxophone, his books, and trinkets that would all be set up in his new room, was heartbreaking.

I felt like a piece of my heart left and there was nothing I could do about it. During the months between signing over custody and physically moving him, I rarely talked to my husband, so I felt like I had to handle it all on my own.

Since Alex left for deployment, we talked less and less, and when we did it involved discussions on his behalf of why we were better off apart and that he was preferring to be single and on his own. I wasn't happy in the marriage either; at least that was something we could agree upon.

It was becoming increasingly clear that all the time we had spent apart created a divide between us. We had grown and matured as individuals within ourselves over the years due to so much time spent apart, but we both failed to grow together in our marriage and our opposite personalities became combative.

At the end of July, we mutually decided to separate and that we would file for divorce upon his return from deployment.

I wasn't sure how to feel about it because at times I felt heartbroken, sometimes I felt justified and confident in the decision, and sometimes I felt worthless wondering how I could be going down this road again.

...

Six hours later, the crystal blue waters and white sandy beaches were shimmering in the sunlight as my plane descended toward Cancun.

Thank God, because I have been sitting in this window seat and have had to pee for the last three and a half hours!

I was too shy to wake up the two people sitting next to me who were peacefully sleeping. Binge-watching *Jane the Virgin* was supposed to calm my nerves about driving a rental car and keep my mind off having to pee but alas, it did not.

The plane landed, and everyone was moving at turtle speed. You would think that all these tourists would have been excited to be there and would leave the plane quickly, but no! It took FOREVER.

When it was finally time for me to get up out of my seat, I stood up so fast that I quickly forgot about how low the overhead bin was. I hit the top of my head hard against the panel. Everyone saw it. Literally everyone. My face was beet red, my head was pounding, and at that point I prayed that I didn't hit the flight attendant call button, because that would have enhanced the embarrassing experience tenfold.

After making my way off the plane with a throbbing headache, I saw that the customs line wasn't terribly long. I opted to hold my pee a little longer and go through customs first.

Big mistake. Huge mistake, actually.

The line came to a standstill. After what seemed like five hours (it was actually fifteen minutes) I made it through customs and literally jogged—if I ran as fast as I would have liked to, I would have surely pissed myself—to find a restroom. There weren't any in sight. I jogged further down toward baggage claim. Of course, the one restroom I did find had a line. After waiting in line for an hour (more like three minutes), I was finally relieved.

Well, let me clarify. I was relieved that I no longer had to pee. I was not relieved, however, from the impending rental car pickup which meant I would officially be driving soon.

In Cancun International Airport, there is a second screening through customs where you take your bags and get to a checkpoint where you press a red button and a light above it will either show green or red.

A short, heavyset woman motioned me toward the checkpoint. "Ma'am, step forward and press the button."

I pressed the button with a smile on my face.

I've surely made it through all the obstacles that this trip is going to throw at me by now. If the light above it shows green, I walk through, ready to take on my trip and bask in the beautiful sun. I'll see that little bar outside the airport door, hear the upbeat music, and relish the fact that I'm back in one of my favorite places in the world.

Suddenly, the most blaring, vibrant, bright red light started shining.

Is this really happening? Seriously? Of course, this is happening! This has been a trip full of deviations, why on earth would it stop with the plane?

To be fair, to everyone else it looked like a normal red light, indicating that they were randomly selected for further screening.

To me, because of everything that had gone wrong so far, it may as well have been setting off sirens, flashing brightly, with a big booming voice over the loudspeaker saying "Alert! Alert! Corrupt luggage alert! Please step to the side!" because that's what it sure felt like.

The security guard pointed me over to a secondary screening area where I needed to get my bags searched. A tall, lanky gentleman wearing glasses started searching my bag. His name tag read Matteo, and I giggled because that was the name of the little boy in the show *Jane the Virgin* that I watched on my flight.

Trying to make light of the situation, I pointed to my backpack, and asked, "Hey, um, you don't happen to see a black bathing suit in there, do you? I thought I packed it and I was looking for it earlier and…"

He looked up at me with a blank stare and stone face, rolled his eyes, looked back at me, gave me the long blink, and then looked back down to continue to search my backpack.

God, I feel like a complete idiot. Why did I ask that? And he not only gave me the eye roll, but did he seriously just long blink at me? How embarrassing! C'mon, Matteo!

Matteo finished checking my bag and handed it back to me. He never did tell me if he found my bathing suit during this search.

"Muchas gracias, Señor Matteo," I said while sliding my backpack over my shoulders and heading toward the airport exit door.

Because of my last minute need to book a rental car for this trip, Patty pulled some strings and was able to set me up with a rental car company that she knew and trusted. She told me that when I exited the airport, to look for someone holding a sign with my last name on it.

As I walked through the airport door, the intense heat from the sun hit my face and I welcomed it.

Finally, I'm here. Let's hope the rest of this trip goes smoothly.

There was upbeat Spanish music playing at the little airport bar. People gathered, drinking cocktails and beer, and there was a sea of people holding up signs with names on them. As great as a margarita sounded after the way my day went, I was going to be driving, so a Coke was the next best refreshing option.

There were buses and taxis galore and I had lost count how many times random people came up to offer me a ride.

I patiently walked through the crowd, looking for a sign that said "Mosher." I circled around at least four times and I couldn't find it.

Of course, this is happening. Why wouldn't it? Just my luck.

I had an internet signal and used Facebook Messenger to call Patty. She said she would call the rental car company and get back to me.

I walked over toward the bar, pulled a cigarette out of my purse, lit it, and inhaled. I closed my eyes and welcomed the nicotine.

Please, little cigarette, please calm my nerves.

It was an "in case of an emotional emergency" pack of cigarettes, and the moment purely justified smoking just one.

Okay, who am I kidding? It was more than one.

My phone rang.

"Hi Patty, any luck?"

"Yes! You have to walk over to the 'Family and Friends' section of the airport. He's been waiting there this whole time."

Family and friends? I looked around and saw the "Family and Friends" sign about twenty feet away from me. *Figures.*

"Ah yes, I see it. I'll head over that way now. I'm sorry for the confusion!"

"Oh no, don't worry, Tiffany! I'll see you soon!"

I walked over to find the sign guy and he drove me to the rental car facility.

My rental car was a little white Chevrolet Malibu. It was quite cute actually and I was glad I spent the extra ten dollars to get an automatic versus a manual transmission. I can drive a stick shift, but it had been quite a while since I had driven one and I wasn't about to go experiment with it in a foreign country.

I sat in the driver's seat, placed the key in the ignition, and started the car. Mariachi music started blasting at such a high volume that I nearly jumped out of my skin.

Crap! Where's the volume button? Everyone is staring at me! Where the hell is it?

My eyes widened as I looked around frantically for the volume button because people were most definitely wondering why I was pretending that I was at the club and having a dance party in the middle of a rental car parking lot.

I quickly turned the music down, adjusted my mirrors, and laughed. Thinking back on everything that had happened so far that day, and how everything went wrong in little ways, I realized that despite all that, I made it there safe and was perfectly fine.

Did I like the feeling of being stressed out? Not at all. I started thinking about forgetting my bathing suit, spilling my tea, hitting my head on the plane, getting stopped in customs, and the excruciatingly loud music in the car. I smiled and started to look at everything from a positive perspective versus nervousness and stress. When I decided to "go with the flow," I felt like it all didn't seem so bad. Those little moments that went wrong, those deviations in the plan, were all shaping the experience to be a fun and memorable chapter of my life.

Besides, it was healthy that I could laugh at myself!

Looking at those moments in a comical sense no longer had me worried about what was going to happen next; rather, I became curious and excited to see what else was going to happen that would add to the crazy adventure I was on.

I put my sunglasses on, turned the Spanish music up to a volume that was just a tiny bit louder than my driving volume back home, made sure my car doors were locked, and started to head toward Nuevo Durango with confidence and a smile.

CHAPTER ELEVEN

FOSTERING HOPE

———

Damn the drivers in Mexico are aggressive.

I'm not an aggressive driver. I'm one of those people who will let two people merge over into my lane because I feel like a bad citizen if I don't. So, needless to say, I had white knuckles gripping the steering wheel while trying to avoid being hit by other vehicles. As I approached a red stoplight, the two-lane highway became a five-lane free-for-all, like we were all on the starting line of a race with no finish line in common.

The air conditioning struggled to keep the car cool in the late August sun. To my left, there was a guy on a black motorcycle who I could literally touch if I were to reach my arm outside of my window. To my right, there was a red car with two young men, both intently staring at me with devious eyes. The driver licked his lips in a way to try to seduce me.

For fuck's sake, really? That's not going to work. Do guys really think that works?

Still trying to be a good citizen in a foreign country, I opted to just roll my eyes instead of giving him the finger. I made sure my car doors were locked again just in case. I tried to remember the karate moves I learned back in sixth grade.

Why won't this light turn green?

I could see in my peripheral vision that their eyes were still burning into me, but I just vowed to remain confident and unaffected by their gestures. Cartels are a known entity in Mexico, and at that moment I was an easy target to follow and possibly run off the road. I had to keep calm and focused.

The light turned green, and in an effort to look cool, the creepy guy spun his tires and sped off down the road. I breathed a sigh of relief.

I got myself into a rhythm and flow of driving and I started to feel more confident. The music was upbeat and fun with all the mariachi vibes and Spanish language that was still too hard for me to translate. The windows were rolled down a little, inviting the ocean breeze of the Riviera Maya into my hair and onto my skin. I had one hand on the wheel while the other danced along to the rhythm of the music.

I noticed the traffic slowing down ahead at a police checkpoint. As each vehicle approached the checkpoint, they slowed down, and the police waved them through.

There were two cars ahead of me as I neared the checkpoint. The car in front of me, a red beaten up looking thing, got waved through.

Please let me go through.

I started to approach the checkpoint, and the cop, who had arm muscles literally the size of my thigh, walked over and stood directly in front of the car, holding his hand out to make me stop. Muscles was carrying a large AK-47 type of firearm, and he started slowly walking toward my driver side door.

Oh no. What did I do? Why is he stopping me? I don't have drugs in my car, do I? Oh my God, what if someone planted drugs in my car? Was it that jerk back at the stop light? Does he have anything to do with this? He waved everyone else through! No other cars had to stop. Am I going to jail? I don't know enough Spanish to get myself out of jail!

Okay, breathe.

As anyone else who just got stopped by the Mexican police would do, I did the first natural instinctive thing that came to mind—I grabbed the Coke that I had sitting in the center console with my right hand and took a huge swig of it while my left hand attempted to flatten my wind-blown hair, as if for some reason that would help things.

"Hola, señor," I said to Mr. Bulging Biceps with a smile. And then I let out a small burp because of the Coke. My eyes widened behind my sunglasses in embarrassment.

Did I seriously just burp at a cop?

This stuff only happens to me, I swear. But I digress.

Time had officially stood still. Traffic was backing up behind us and it seemed like I had been sitting there for minutes. Mr. Mega Muscular Macho Man stared me down through his sunglasses a little longer than necessary in my opinion as his right hand stroked the side of the firearm.

"Solo revisando su cinturón de seguridad." He told me that he was just checking my seat belt.

Sure you are, buddy.

I smiled sweetly. "Si, tengo mi cinturón de seguridad," I said as I pulled on the seat belt twice for extra emphasis. I could see right through the bullshit but decided to play his game. I had to stay confident and act like I knew what I was doing. I knew without a doubt he saw my seat belt across my body when I pulled up. He stepped away from the car and waved me through the checkpoint.

Look out world, Tiffany is officially badass!

I turned the music back up, laughed as I hit the side of the steering wheel with my hand a couple times, let the wind blow through my hair, and drove on toward the jungle.

The skies ahead were incredibly dark. Lightning flashed across the sky and I was headed straight toward it. Being one who absolutely loves and is turned on by thunderstorms (yes, I said turned on; big deal, thunderstorms are awesome!), I started to get even more excited.

I noticed that the closer I got to the jungle, there were ropes that stretched across the highway about every half-mile or so for monkeys to cross. I didn't see any monkeys, but I constantly kept eye out. Further down the road, I passed a jaguar-crossing sign which was slightly scary yet enticing.

Jaguars? Please let me see a jaguar. From far away. But close enough for me to, like, SEE it. But seriously though, far away.

The sky was getting darker by the minute. The wind whipped the trees, but the rain hadn't started yet. The sky was quite ominous and I prayed that the rain would hold off until I got to my destination.

Forty minutes later, I arrived at the village. As soon as I pulled up to the house of Enrique, my village host, the rain started pouring down, turning the dirt roads of the village into pools of mud.

Thank God I got here when I did! It's a monsoon!

Patty, her husband Hansel, Marcz, the music teacher in the village, Enrique, and his family were all sitting on the front porch of his home. The bright orange walls inside the bamboo-covered porch invited me in and the brightly colored Mayan mural of a woman on the wall was a symbol of the rich culture that Nuevo Durango represents.

Map of the village of Nuevo Durango.

We sat on the porch together, talked about our plans for the school restoration project, and ate a late lunch that was authentically Mayan and farm-to-table with rich, fragrant, seasoned chicken, rice, beans, handmade tortillas, and hibiscus water. The deep dark pink hibiscus water was a pleasant thirst quencher. I normally don't like fruit juices, but the taste was heavenly, resembling a dark cherry flavor.

After lunch, the rain was still pouring down.

"Cheers to Tiffany, la Princesa de la Lluvia!" Enrique said as he held up his glass.

"La Princesa de la Lluvia? What does that mean?" I asked. *La princesa. A princess of some kind. I do love the sound of that!*

"The Princess of the Rain. It's normally the dry season here but you brought us some much-needed rain for my farm," Enrique explained.

"Well, sure, I'll take the credit. Rain Princess. I like it!" I smiled and we all laughed.

Note to self: add Rain Princess to my resume when I get home.

Marcz, Enrique, and I decided to play guitar together. We played a medley of songs, including "House of the Rising Sun" and "La Bamba." One of the young Mayan girls in the village, who was learning how to play guitar in Marcz's music class, came over and wanted to play with me. I showed her the chords to one of my favorite songs by the Avett Brothers, "The Fall", and we played it together. Even though she didn't speak any English and I barely spoke any Spanish, music was the language that brought us together that afternoon.

After two hours of playing guitar and singing, the rain let up. Patty, Marcz, and I walked over to the kindergarten school to discuss "Fostering Hope," the school restoration project that AIDNOW and Dreams for Mayan Children were partnering for. The small, one-room concrete building had dirty white walls and a red roof. There was a gravel walking path that led from the road to the school and trees, large sharp jagged rocks, and overgrown grass and weeds to the left and right of the path.

We discussed ideas on clearing out the sharp rocks and vegetation, leveling out the land, expanding the concrete entrance to the school, and placing in a concrete walkway from the road to the school. I couldn't wait to get the project started because the children needed a safe place to play and learn.

The site of the AIDNOW and Dreams for Mayan Children
school restoration project, the Francisco Gonzalez
Bocanegra Preescolar, in Nuevo Durango, Mexico.

It was a little past sunset and the village was quiet, aside from the playful growling of four stray dogs that were playing and roughhousing. By 8:30 p.m., I was purely exhausted. I retreated to my cabaña, a little bamboo hut with a full-size bed complete with a properly constructed mosquito net.

Oh yay! I don't have to worry about this one falling down on me like the one in Puerto Rico!

The rain from earlier in the day cooled the air. Wearing only a sports bra and a pair of shorts, I was comfortable.

I couldn't believe that I was so nervous just hours prior at the airport. While lying in my bed, I thought about how confident I felt once I made it past each of the little hurdles of the day and that confidence gave me strength. I felt stronger because I focused on the positive things rather than stuff that made me feel anxious or scared.

Being out there in the jungle with just the basic necessities, displaced from normal day-to-day life, felt so freeing and therapeutic. I thought back to my time in Puerto Rico. Each time that I was in a situation where I had to live more simply and with less than what I was used to in my daily life, I was reminded of what really matters the most. Being in the presence of good company, having the flexibility to adapt, and feeling purpose made life feel sweeter and more fulfilling.

The remote darkness swallowed my hut, amplifying the nighttime sounds of the jungle. The mix of insects, frogs, dogs barking in the distance, and some weird grunting sound that seemed to be right outside of my window lulled me into a deep sleep.

The next morning, I was awakened by the sounds of roosters crowing and dogs barking. I reached for my phone to see what time it was.

What the heck is this green goopy stuff?

The remnants of what used to be some sort of insect were smeared into the bed sheet. Judging by the brownish-green guts and one still-intact wing, it no doubt was the unfortunate outcome of a hitchhiker that landed on me in the middle of the night when I went to the bathroom.

Figures. Sorry, dude.

At that point, seeing the bug guts didn't really bother me at all; in fact, it was a fun reminder that I was actually waking up in a Mayan village. How often can people say that?

I looked at the time on my phone.

6:08 a.m.? I need tea, like now.

I climbed out of the mosquito net and went into the bathroom.

"Well, well. Of course you would sit on the toilet when I have to pee," I said sarcastically to the little brown lizard that had taken refuge on the toilet seat as if it could understand me. I gently tapped it and it leapt onto the floor. As I took a cool shower, I could see the lizard staring at me with one eye while slowly waving its tail from its spot next to the toilet.

"Are you seducing me this early in the morning?" I jokingly asked out loud.

Oh my God, did I just ask a lizard if it was seducing me? I need caffeine.

After the quick shower, I bid adieu to the lizard and headed out to see if anyone else was awake. As I suspected, I was the only one walking about the dirt roads. Two brown dogs decided to escort me as I walked, playing and chasing each other, competing to walk closest to me. I turned left down another gravel road to a part of the village I hadn't been to yet.

The large trees towered over me and little huts line the road. Colorful clothing was laid out on lines to dry and baby chickens were scattered in the front yards, pecking at the ground. The dogs ran past me in a frenzy and into the woods. I kept walking on the road and came to a clearing where there was a museo de insectos, or insect museum, which displayed different insects found in that region of Mexico.

Suddenly, I heard intense growling and rustling in the surrounding woods coming right toward me.

I automatically thought of the jaguar crossing sign that I saw while driving there and accepted my fate.

This is it. Is this the way I meet my doom? By getting eaten by a freaking jaguar?

I looked frantically around to see where and what the wild animal was. The growling got closer, and the two dogs that were walking with me before ran out of the woods.

"Oh, thank God!" I said as I petted them, grateful that as long as these two were there, I should be safe.

OUCH! What in the world?

All of a sudden, I felt a harsh pinching sensation right under my shorts on my left hip. I pulled the side of my shorts down to see a small black spider that had its teeth buried into me. For a little guy, he sure could pack a punch. I grabbed him and threw him away from me, noticing two small puncture wounds.

Great. I'm gonna have to keep an eye on this.

I licked my finger and wiped away the small amount of blood.

Two hours later, I was driving back to Cancun so I could fly home. The trip was short and sweet and focused only on project planning. I was thankful for the little deviations in the plans that made that trip special and unique.

Years ago, the things that went wrong on that trip would have given me immense stress and anxiety because I'm naturally a planner, a coordinator, and I thrive on routine. However, as I learned to embrace the little challenges and laugh at myself along the way, I found myself also embracing the moments of stress. I realized that when things don't go as planned, they give me an opportunity to shift my mindset and handle them with positivity. Those disruptive moments, those feelings of stress, those shifts in attitude; they helped me grow stronger and more confident.

Plus, they just make for some damn good stories.

As the plane ascended into the early afternoon sun, I closed my eyes and smiled as I thought back on the events of that crazy whirlwind weekend. It was time to go home and get back to reality, prepare for the upcoming fall months with the kids going back to school, start another graduate class, and of course, the holidays. I was ready to go home and approach those inevitable life events and could do so with freedom and ease.

As the deployment continued, Alex and I tried our best to get along for the sake of communicating about the kids. However, I knew that when he got back, life was going to drastically change. I felt very nervous about the thought of starting my life completely over again at almost forty years old.

After the trip to Mexico, I was incredibly inspired and motivated to push myself even harder to do something drastic, scary, and empowering. Call it an addiction to finding confidence if you will. It felt good to gain confidence, and I wanted more of it.

I wanted to travel solo again, far away, and of course include volunteering somehow. There was no need to spend tons of time researching and weighing different options for places to travel.

I already knew where I was going to go.

PART THREE

SHE'S BACK!

CHAPTER TWELVE

THE HEAD VS. THE HEART

———

Bring on the snow-capped mountains, the gorgeous views, the amazing food and tea, and the incredible culture!

Okay, yes, that could literally be numerous places on this great vast Earth of ours. But I had one particular place in mind that is in a league of its own.

Pack your bag, my friend! We are headed to Nepal!

When I mentioned to family and friends that I wanted to go to Nepal, I can't tell you how many times they asked if I was going to go on a trek or climb Mt. Everest. I barely made the hike up Old Rag Mountain in the Shenandoah Mountains a few years ago, let alone even attempt a trek. No, hiking was not what I envisioned when I pictured myself being in Nepal.

What I envisioned was being in some little remote village in the middle of nowhere, experiencing culture, learning from the local people, drinking Nepalese tea, enjoying the sights and smells of someplace new and different, all while contributing to a cause much bigger than me.

Having found solace and personal growth in my previous volunteer trips, I knew that I couldn't visit Nepal without a purpose. I applied to All Hands and Hearts again and got accepted to volunteer in late January 2020 for two weeks at their Marin earthquake recovery program, which involved rebuilding schools that were destroyed in the 2015 earthquake.

This Nepal trip is very well-timed because I need a freaking break from reality! Just for a little bit.

Don't get me wrong; I love my kids dearly. I actually love my job and my coworkers. I just felt emotionally heavy at the time and I needed to escape for a little bit so I could collect my thoughts.

I've lost count of how many times during the deployment that I felt trapped. It wasn't Alex's fault. I enabled myself to feel that way. I felt like I was suffocating in my home. His presence was very strong due to memories we made there. Plus, all his stuff was still spread throughout the house. There was nothing that I could do but just sit and wait for him to get back so we could get the divorce process rolling.

I knew that I wasn't going to have much Wi-Fi while in Nepal, and I was looking forward to having ample time to reflect.

Do I want to try to stay in my marriage for the sake of the kids but risk my mental health? With everything that I've had to sacrifice in my life as a military spouse and a mother, do I want to take control of my life now and be the one to make the decisions of where I go? How can I be the best mom and role model to my children if I'm unhappy, depressed, sad, and constantly retreating from everyone? I have all these questions but the major one is this: Do I stay in my marriage or not? I'm hoping that while I'm in Nepal, the answer will become clear to me.

...

Ah, homecoming day. It was late January 2020. The long-awaited/
long-overdue/but-am-I-ready-for-this homecoming day had
arrived. My trip to Nepal was scheduled for three days later.

My bags were already fully packed. Hell, they were packed
for at least three weeks prior to the trip. I had this unnerving
fear that I was going to forget something important.

Elora, Mason, and I were waiting at the Navy base for
Alex's flight to arrive. It was late in the evening and the cold
brisk air and wind was telling of possible snowfall on the
horizon. It didn't end up snowing but it sure as hell felt cold
enough for it to. I was incredibly nervous. So, what did I do?
Even though I knew we would be parting ways after his return,
I did what any woman would do when she was nervous about
seeing an ex; dress to impress.

*I am FREEZING! I should have worn my hat. But no! I
had to try to look sexy and hot for this homecoming! Note to
self: find a way to force my hat to look sexy!*

*I just have to see how I feel when I see his face for the first
time in ten months.*

As soon as I saw him walk off the plane and toward the
three of us, there weren't any feelings of excitement or relief
like I had felt during past deployment homecomings.

I felt nothing.

Don't get me wrong, it was great to see him and have
him back safe and sound. It was wonderful that the kids were
excited and happy to see him.

I knew in that moment that any sort of hope for recon-
ciliation, if there was any, was gone.

We all got in the car to drive home. I fought back tears.
Thank God it was dark out so nobody could see them. I

needed something to pick up the mood. Elora, having taken an extreme interest in the Broadway play *Hamilton*, had memorized all the lyrics. I pulled up the songs on Spotify so that we could listen to her sing along.

All I can think right now is of the battle going on between my head and my heart. I do care for him as a person and have respect for him as the father of my son. But I can't help the feelings of sadness that are taking over me.

I can't relate to my husband anymore.

CHAPTER THIRTEEN

ADRENALINE: A BLESSING AND A CURSE

———

The thought of traveling alone all the way across the world literally scares the shit out of me.

To the outside world, when I talked about my travel plans and told people that I was going to help build schools, they heard the excitement in my voice, like a fearless woman who felt like she could take on the world.

Deep down, I was petrified.

Expressing confidence to my coworkers, family, and friends temporarily made the fear subside. When I thought about the journey, though, I couldn't help but think that maybe I took on something too big.

I can cancel. I can give into the fear but where would that leave me? It would leave Nepal on the bucket list, still unaccomplished. I know that I need to take the opportunity to travel there now before my life takes a crazy turn. Suck it up, Buttercup!

Having been through divorce before, I knew that my options for travel could potentially be limited because I was going to be a single mom. I also knew that I had to stay mentally focused and strong because my first divorce crippled me tremendously and led me to a deep depression. And there was no way in hell that I was going to let that happen again.

...

I'm seriously doing this! I'm going to Nepal! But I need to find something to eat, like NOW. I'm getting hangry! (Insert RBF, or "resting bitch face," here.)

Despite the excitement and nervousness of finally being on my way to Nepal, a tiny bit of crankiness was starting to build up while waiting for my next flight during my layover in Philadelphia. My blood sugar level was dropping, and I started to feel a headache and dizziness coming on because I hadn't eaten in a few hours. Pure fear had also fully kicked in.

To prepare for my twelve-hour flight to Doha, Qatar, I decided to eat one last American meal and ordered a burger and some fries. Not just any burger though; a Spicy Baja burger from Smashburger.

What am I thinking? Should I really be eating jalapenos on a burger this close to a twelve-hour flight when I'm already feeling nervous? But this burger—this juicy, flavorful, spicy burger—oh my God is it the ultimate comfort food or what? Oh, and I better use the bathroom like twelve times before I get trapped in my window seat.

Eh, make that thirteen times just to be on the safe side.

As I walked aboard the plane, I could feel my fear slipping away. The airline, Qatar Airways, had this very soft piano music playing and there was a pink hue in the lighting all throughout the plane. It felt very welcoming and the crew was so pleasant.

I sat in a seat that had extra leg room. Next to me was a mother with her infant, a little girl that was maybe about five or six months old. I am normally a very patient person so having the baby next to me was not a stressful thing at all. The baby was looking at me with her wide brown eyes and she was smiling at me as she handed me little her little toy. I handed it back to her. She dropped it on the floor and looked at me, so I picked it up and handed it back to her. Let's just say this cycle repeated itself about twenty times, but she was so cute, and I had nothing else to do, so I didn't mind at all.

After the baby decided that I was boring and found a bottle of milk more interesting, I decided to buy some Wi-Fi so I could text my kids, family, and friends via WhatsApp, and scroll through Facebook to pass the time.

Okay, so if I stay awake for a few hours, render myself completely exhausted, then pop a melatonin, I should be able to get a bunch of sleep on the last leg of the flight and then the time zone difference won't affect me! Yep, sounds like a solid plan to me.

It always works out that way, doesn't it?

"Ms. Mosher? Your Hindi meal, ma'am," the stewardess said with a smile as she handed me a small rectangular tray.

"Oh, excuse me? My what?"

She sensed my obvious confusion. "Yes ma'am, you pre-ordered a Hindi meal for this flight."

Her smile is so genuine. I need to make a mental note to smile like her more because I've been told that my RBF can be quite strong.

"Oh, I did? Awesome! Okay thank you!"

Well, this is a fun surprise! I sure don't remember ordering a Hindi meal when I booked the flight, but hey, I enjoy trying new foods so what the heck? Let's see what this is all about.

I opened the aluminum foil top and glanced inside the packaging.

Okay, I see rice. I see meat and a red sauce. Oh my God it smells amazing. What is this even called?

The flavor was incredible, unlike anything I had ever tasted before. When I pictured in my mind what Middle Eastern food would taste like, it was that exact meal. I couldn't quite put my finger on what the spices were, but it did have a kick to it. The meal got me more and more excited to go to a different area of the world that I have never traveled to.

About three hours into the flight (around 11:30 p.m. EST) I started to feel tired. However, for the life of me I could not get comfortable in my seat. It was difficult for me to get positioned right without some part of my body going numb. As I restlessly fidgeted in my seat, I couldn't help but envy the peaceful slumber of the mother and infant sitting next to me.

That woman... Pure magic. Look at her, all contorted into some crazy position so that the baby can sleep. The circulation in her left arm and right leg surely must be gone. How is she sleeping so soundly and here I am, unable to even get somewhat comfortable?

To say I was a tiny bit envious is an understatement.

But then, it hit me. It had been so long since I had an infant to care for. That's just what mothers do.

I was finally able to get a very broken six hours of sleep and was woken up by the stewardesses bringing brunch around. Brunch was another Middle Eastern meal. It was very delicious, consisting of tea, spicy scrambled eggs with chicken meatballs, roasted potatoes, pepper relish, a croissant, fruit, and yogurt.

Three hours later, at 4:30 p.m. local time, we landed in Doha.

Finally! Hallelujah! I can stretch my legs! And I REALLY need to pee.

I had a ten-hour layover ahead of me. I also had a shit ton of homework to do for my International Law and US Security Policy course, a subject I admit that I was not excited to study because the material was so dry. At the same time, I knew that I was about to be without stable Wi-Fi in the mountains for two weeks so I couldn't rely on having time later to complete the assignments.

Finding the motivation to tackle the homework was, well, not exactly the easiest thing to do. The fact that I had about ten hours of international law homework ahead of me was mentally exhausting, especially after not sleeping well on the flight. I knew I needed to get somewhere comfortable but everywhere throughout the airport was very crowded and noisy. I also couldn't find a seat that had an outlet close by.

I saw a lounge up on the second floor which was my saving grace. I was able to buy access to it. For a minute there, I felt so classy. As I entered the lounge, I was amazed at the beautiful sights.

A buffet? Unlimited drinks? Cozy and comfortable seating? Outlet plugs everywhere? Showers? Wait, are those people in that dimly lit room over there laying down and sleeping? They are sleeping! On a flat surface! This is going to be the best fifty-five dollars I've spent in a long time.

I stood outside of the windows looking into the dark lounge room. To everyone else, I probably looked like a little lost puppy sitting outside of a house in the freezing cold, looking into the window and seeing its family sitting by the warm fire.

Immediately the conflicting voices in my head started going to work.

First, the envious one.

That could be me in there, catching up on sleep on an actual flat surface, but no! I have to do this damn international law homework. Why did I even sign up for this class? Why did I bother to bring my laptop? It made my backpack like thirty pounds heavier. Uuuugghhhh.

Second, the academic one striving for excellence.

But Tiffany, you are a good student who has goals! You are achieving dreams! It's just a little bit of homework; knock it out and take a nap later! You got this!

Of course, the mockingly judgmental one too.

Why did you even take on this course when you knew, you KNEW, you wouldn't be able to work on it for two weeks while you were on this trip? You're an idiot.

Seriously? Miss 'Oh, if I take this course and just push myself tirelessly, I can finish my degree program in August versus October?' Miss 'I have no idea how I'm going to do this but I'm going to find a way?' Miss 'I will just figure it out?'

Let's not forget the sleepy voice of reason!

You can't be serious. Look at those people sleeping! YOU could be SLEEPING. Flat. On a flat surface. SLEEPING FLAT ON A FLAT SURFACE. Forget the homework.

Following up is that annoyingly encouraging voice.

Soak in your surroundings! You're in Qatar! Eat some food, make some tea! You enjoy writing! You'll knock out the homework in no time!

And finally, the one that thinks sleep is the best (or only) option.

You know what? I'm done! I'm tired. I got crappy sleep on that flight. I earned my right to rest! I can actually go in there, lay down FLAT, and take a nap. I'm going to be volunteering and working my ass off for the next two weeks! To hell with all this homework!

Defiant as ever, I walked directly over to the coffee station, made a cup of tea, found an empty seat, opened my laptop and plugged in the charger. I then grabbed my notebook and flash drive and glared at my computer and international law case study that I needed to analyze in absolute disgust.

And for the next eight hours straight, I knocked out five assignments that were due.

CHAPTER FOURTEEN

NAMASTE, KATHMANDU!

———

Who was I kidding before? I was never going to just throw the homework I needed to do out the window.

I know I have obligations, and, in the grand scheme of things, I actually like to learn.

Yes, I can begrudgingly admit I liked learning about international law.

But in the end, after wrapping up all those assignments, I felt invigorated and at ease with myself because I achieved my goal to finish them. I knew that if I had put them off and opted for sleep, they would have distracted me too much from the work I was going to be doing out there.

I need a shower. One last hot shower.

After I completed my homework, I found the shower in the women's restroom. Let me tell you, the shower in the women's restroom in the Oryx Lounge at Hamad International Airport was the best shower I had taken in years. The water pressure? Freaking divine. Decor? So classy and elegant with the gold colored accents. The shampoo and conditioner? Smelled heavenly and accurately addressed the tangles of my airplane hair aftermath.

I took a much longer shower than I needed to, but I felt like I earned it after all the homework I did. Not having a hairdryer, I combed my wet hair and pulled it back into a braid. I felt so clean, incredibly exhausted, and yet buzzing with adrenaline.

Two in the morning approached and it was almost time to board my flight to Kathmandu.

Am I really doing this? I'm going to be in Nepal in a few hours. Ahhhh!

About four hours into the flight and three cups of tea, the girl sitting next to me tapped me to get my attention. As I turned toward her to see what she wanted, she pointed out the window. No words were needed.

There we were, eye level with the top of the Himalayan mountains in the sky. The view of those massive snow-capped mountains was incredibly breathtaking. My jaw dropped.

My God, this is absolutely beautiful. I'm in awe. I can't stop staring. I can't believe that there is something this big and so vast in the world. To be this high in the sky and at eye level with these massive mountains—honestly words can't describe it. I can't believe that I'm actually here on a completely different continent thousands of miles away from home.

About an hour later, we landed at Tribhuvan International Airport.

Prior to landing, there was a flood of emotions I experienced when they said we were about to descend.

Can I navigate this all by myself? Can I handle this? I have to find a taxi. I need to buy a SIM card. I have to get my tourist visa and exchange my money. Will they speak English? Ugh, I have no choice but to face it, though. I am just going to have to roll with the punches.

I noticed when the plane landed that I was not as nervous as I thought I was going to be.

As I walked off the plane and smelled the air, my mind was calm and steady.

I can do this. I'm here! I'm finally here. Okay, let's do this.

I got my tourist visa, went through customs and immigration, and then approached the currency exchange counter. The funny thing about the money was that I didn't know how much I was going to need. Anyone that knows me well knows that I'm not good at math.

"Next," a short and skinny gentleman with a head full of dark hair yelled from the counter.

"I need to exchange American dollars, please."

He stared at me with a blank face, like he had been sitting at the counter for the past two days straight without a break. "How many American dollars?"

Dammit. Math. I didn't do the math! I absolutely hate math. I'm the worst at math! Why didn't I plan out the math beforehand?

In a state of panic, I gave the gentleman $330.00, which converted to about 36,300 rupees.

Apparently, that must have been a lot of rupees based on his facial expression that read "Are you kidding me?" He looked at me like I was crazy. His eyes basically said, "Why are you getting this many? Do you even know where you are? You're never gonna spend this much money." He shook his head and handed me the massive wad of bills.

For the first time ever, I felt rich holding that large amount of money and I felt ready to take on Nepal! And no, not to find some club in Kathmandu and "make it rain."

I found my suitcase with the "Avett Brothers At the Beach" luggage tag (of course I had to take the Avett Brothers with me somehow!) in baggage claim and made my way to the Nepal Telecom kiosk to get my SIM card for my cell phone. Afterward, I arranged for a taxi.

That taxi ride, well, was the most insane ride (well, car ride) I've ever been on in my life.

I sat on an Aladdin-like magic carpet in the backseat of a Jeep. We were flying through the mass chaos of the city of Kathmandu. There were cars coming from the left and zooming in from the right. There were tons of scooters as well; sometimes with two or three people on each. Toddlers and infants were even on the scooters being held tight by their adult rider. Everything was going in all sorts of directions—it was very organized chaos.

I was expecting to see people crash at any moment. Horns were honking and people and cows were just walking aimlessly in the streets. As we drove down a side alley, I felt like we were going to run over at least twenty people while flying at what felt like a top speed, even though it probably wasn't. It was wild. I had never experienced anything like that, and I was just basically holding on to the back doorknob with white knuckles, hoping and praying I would survive the ride.

We stopped at a traffic light and I was breathing heavy, as if I had just run a marathon (I'm really not trying to be dramatic, this was just all new to me). I looked up and saw a huge monkey sitting there on top of a building—in the middle of Kathmandu! It was unbelievable, yet incredibly exciting. One thing I noticed was that there were a lot of signs written in English and a lot of people I encountered spoke English. The uneasiness about the language barrier quickly dissipated, which was really nice.

After the twenty-five-minute crazy taxi ride, I finally made it to the Kumari Boutique Hotel. Tucked back off the busy streets of Thamel, the tourist area of Kathmandu, the slightly ajar large wooden door welcomed me in along with the small Buddha statue on the wall and the smell of incense inside the small lobby. It was simple and quaint.

This. Is. Perfect!

I was shown to my room on the second floor. I got excited when I saw a tea kettle and some Nepali tea bags sitting neatly next to it in a little white dish. By now, you know me and my love for tea. I couldn't wait to try it!

As I sat there, sipping on the decadent tea and looking out the window, I was still in disbelief that I was in Nepal. The afternoon setting sun was trying to hide behind the buildings and I could see hundreds of yellow, green, red, white, and blue Nepali prayer flags waving in the breeze. The relief I felt was such a joy.

I can't believe I made it this far. The plane with its smooth jazz and sleepy baby, the lounge with my two sides battling it out and the get-it-done side winning, the scramble to get my luggage and a SIM card and exchange my currency, and finally the most INSANE people-swarming-the-streets taxi ride I've ever been a part of have all led me here: looking out this window, ready to volunteer. It feels almost like a dream.

Careful not to mess up the sleep I was going to get that evening (while lying flat! On a bed!), I took a forty-five-minute nap to gain some energy. A few hours later, around 4:30 p.m., I met up with Sophie.

Sophie was a lovely and sweet woman originally from England. She was spending time in Nepal after traveling from the Philippines and Australia, where she had been living for the past two and a half years. We found each other on the volunteer group Facebook page and arranged to meet in Kathmandu so we could travel together to the volunteer base.

As she showed me around downtown Thamel, I smelled all the amazing food cooking on the street corners and in the restaurants, heard the music from the shops and bars, and couldn't help but glance into the different types of stores that lined the streets. From trekking gear to souvenirs to tea (I made a mental note to make sure to buy tea when I came back through Kathmandu), the stores offered a never-ending plethora of options to choose from.

Nepali prayer flags were everywhere. I never got tired of looking at them. The air was cool and got colder as the afternoon gave into night. Sophie and I ordered dal bhat for dinner. Dal bhat is a typical dish found in Nepal, India and Bangladesh that consists of rice, a lentil soup (the dal), and then vegetables, potatoes, and chicken.

Oh wow, this is quite spicy! Amazingly spicy. Give me more!

After dinner, we were on a mission to buy the perfect pair of Nepali pants to wear at the volunteer base. Sophie helped me barter (okay, she did all the bartering) for some really cool pants that were burnt orange, burgundy, mustard yellow, and hunter green; all the fall colors I love.

It was so comforting to know that I didn't have to spend my first evening all the way across the world alone.

CHAPTER FIFTEEN

AN UNPREDICTABLE JOURNEY TO MARIN

———

I have a riddle for you.

What do you get when you cross extreme fatigue with a night of heat blasting in a tiny hotel room?

Give up?

You get a girl who slept like a rock and who could not care less about other people's opinions of her appearance despite her incredibly dry and parched lips and mouth, static-electricity-induced hair that looked like she stuck her finger in an electrical socket, and the most dehydrated skin covered in a shiny layer of sweat thanks to that unrelenting hotel heater. Even her eyeballs were as dry as the Sahara. But she was rocking it!

...

I wasn't sure if I was going to sleep well due to my arrival adrenaline and the time zone difference, but that heat really knocked me out. I woke up at 5:15 a.m., took a hot shower, and made Sophie and I some tea.

We carried our bags downstairs, and the gentleman working the front desk graciously offered us a complimentary breakfast to-go since we were leaving prior to the dining area opening.

Oh, yum! An apple, croissant, a blueberry muffin, and a juice box! I can't even remember the last time I had a juice box!

What he didn't realize was that by giving me that breakfast, he saved Sophie from dealing with my crankiness later had my blood sugar dropped from not eating. I had just met her. She didn't need to witness that!

The taxi ride wasn't as wild as the day before due to the lack of traffic, but it was still a little chaotic. Getting to the bus stop was quite interesting because it didn't look like a typical bus stop that I was used to seeing in America. The bus stop in Kathmandu was a crowded area with some buses but mostly jeeps or minivans. There were a group of men and women warming their hands over a fire made from burning trash. Other men and women were walking around selling candies and oranges to passersby.

As soon as we stepped out of our cab, a man walked over to me, grabbed my suitcase, and just started walking away with it.

"Where are you going? Where you want to go?" he asked me in broken English while wheeling my suitcase away. I walked quickly after him.

Sophie replied, "Can you take us to Sindhuli, please?"

Her British accent is so cute, I can't stand it!

"Sindhuli?"

"Yes, Sindhuli."

"Yes, come, come, I take you to Sindhuli. You pay here, six hundred rupees," he said as he pointed to an older gentleman with a full beard and mustache standing behind the bus stop counter. Then he pointed toward a seven passenger Jeep and started walking to it.

Sindhuli is a small city about a six-hour drive southeast of Kathmandu and is where we would be meeting with other volunteers to travel to the Marin volunteer base together.

Hoisting my bag up on top of the Jeep, he said, "I put your bag back there. Don't worry, I drive."

Um. Wait, my suitcase! Now what? My suitcase is on top of a Jeep and I am not even sure if I'm going to the right place.

I turned to Sophie. "I guess this is our Jeep?"

"I suppose so!" she replied, rather calmly as he grabbed her rucksack, threw it up top, and secured our bags with rope.

Should I be freaking out? Well, she's not freaking out. Should I be freaking out for the both of us? She seems calm. Okay, Tiffany, act calm.

Sophie was my saving grace because, being used to traveling the world, she didn't seem phased by any of this. Her calming energy helped reduce my stress level.

We paid our bus fare and walked back toward the Jeep.

"Your bag, miss. Your bag," the driver said to me.

"You put my bag up there already, sir," I replied as I pointed up at my suitcase on top of the Jeep.

"No, your bag," he said as he pointed to my backpack.

"Oh no, that's okay, I'll keep my backpack with me in the Jeep."

"No, I put on top. I drive."

"No, honestly, it's okay. I'll hold it."

"No, I put on top with other bags. Don't worry, I drive."

My face surely was telling of my uncertainty with my grimaced look. I was very hesitant because in my backpack, I had my life essentials: my purse, my passport, my money, and my heavy ass laptop.

Why did I bring this damn laptop again?

Oddly enough, and I don't know why, the thing I was stressed about the most was the stupid laptop. I blamed my innate desire to learn on that one.

And then, the dramatic irrational thoughts kicked in.

We are going to hit a major boulder while driving and unbeknownst to me and everyone else in the vehicle, my backpack, yes, only my backpack, with everything I need to be able to leave the country in two weeks, will fly off the top of the Jeep, and plunge into a river below to never be seen again. Not anyone else's bag; just mine. Oh hell no, my backpack is not ending up in some river!

"I would feel much safer if I keep it in my lap."

"I drive, don't worry."

Don't back down. Smile and stay polite.

As I held on to my backpack for dear life, I climbed into the backseat with Sophie.

And then we sat there. And waited. Knowing we had to be in Sindhuli by 2:00 p.m., the clock was quickly approaching 7:30 a.m.

After what seemed like an eternity, four young guys crawled into the Jeep and stuffed themselves into the row in front of us, which was meant to hold three people. Sophie, me, and our backpacks were taking up the backseat.

Sophie and I whispered to each other.

"Should we move our stuff over and let one of them sit with us?" I asked her.

"I think they are fine. Let's just see how the drive goes for now."

The guys talked among themselves and looked back at us, laughing at times. We had no clue what they were saying but it made us giggle.

Luckily, we started the journey to Sindhuli right on time at 7:30 a.m. The driver put on the loudest techno Nepali dance music. Sophie and I couldn't help but laugh because it proved to be an interesting choice of music for that early in the morning.

The smog was very thick as we fist pumped to the music driving through Kathmandu. The visibility was quite low and I could smell the pollution in the air. The streets were very crowded, and more people were burning trash to keep warm. Stores were opening up for the day and the shop owners were preparing their storefronts by laying out handicrafts and clothing.

There were electrical cables everywhere. They came together on street corners in a large black mass of cabling, intertwining together with no organization. Imagine a large rubber band ball. It looked exactly like that, except it was one thousand times bigger and high up on an electrical pole, with cables joining the ball from every street angle imaginable.

What on earth do they do if a cable needs to be fixed? I empathize with you, Mr. Repair Guy, whoever you are. That job has got to be insanely hard.

As we traveled through the morning rush hour traffic, we drove past two large, brown, very healthy-looking cows standing in the middle of the busy street. Yes, cows; just standing there, minding their business and calm as could be. Cars and scooters were driving fast and aggressively but at the same time were being careful to not hit or disturb them in any way.

I remember learning a long time ago that cows are sacred in the Hindu religion and I saw it for the first time in action. In Hinduism, due to her sanctity, the cow must be protected and treated with respect. She represents divinity, grace, and nonviolence. She provides nourishment, is a passive creature, and is a representative of Mother Earth, offering protection to those surrounding her because of her maternal nature.[5]

It was so interesting to see those majestic creatures just standing in the middle of the busy city street, without a care in the world, almost seeming like they didn't mind the chaos going on around them.

Although the time it took us to navigate past the cows was no more than twenty seconds, time seemed to slow down. As we drove past, the techno music faded, almost like we were driving in incredibly slow motion. I looked out the window and was mesmerized by one of the cows. She looked right at me while chewing on something.

I feel...hmm. What exactly is this feeling?

My eyes met with hers.

Connection. I feel connected to her. Not in a creepy way, and not even in a "damn, I could go for a nice big steak or juicy burger" kind of way. Her stoic presence in the middle of a chaotic city street is speaking to me as a reminder that I need to relax, to calm down, and that amidst chaos, beauty can be found anywhere. She is telling me that in times when life can seem much like the streets of Kathmandu, with its craziness, lack of adequate direction, and stressors aggressively coming at me from all directions, that I can find strength within myself, like an anchor. Much like the cow standing firm, confident, and strong, I too can find that solidarity and not let my surroundings define my mental state. While I can't control what is going on around me, I can control my emotions and how I respond.

---

5   *Encyclopaedia Britannica Online*, Academic ed., s.v. "Sanctity of the cow," accessed April 6, 2020.

It was amazing that through something so wildly random and unexpected, I discovered so much about myself. I was consciously aware of my surroundings, kept an open mind, and was able to listen to and feel what the world was trying to tell me. I just needed to be willing to see it, touch it, embrace it, and learn from it.

And just like that, as quickly as time stood still for me to learn this valuable life lesson from her, time sped up again and the cows were just a figure in the distance behind us.

After about an hour and a half of driving, we stopped for our first break. Sophie and I got out of the car to stretch our legs and use the restroom. The toilet was basically a round porcelain hole in the ground. I had never seen anything like it. I knew they were common in Asia, but I had never used one before. The toilet was quite filthy, covered in mud and remains of feces.

Well, okay. I guess I gotta just pop a squat and see how this goes.

As I squatted, I tried my best to make perfect aim because I didn't want to be the person that pissed off my driver because I had to get my backpack out of the backseat (where he clearly did not want my backpack to be) to get a change of clothes.

I noticed there was a large gap in the door where anyone could just look in.

Great! I don't have any toilet paper and I don't have anything else to clean myself off with. Thank God I only had to pee this time. My only option is to twerk. Lovely!

This should come as no surprise, but I'm horrible at twerking. I felt ridiculous as I bounced my ass up and down. I hoped and prayed that nobody was looking in at me.

Mental note, Tiffany: Practice this twerk dance. It can have its benefits back home too!

Luckily, my dignity was spared and so were my pants.

As we all climbed back into the Jeep, Sophie climbed in first, I sat in the middle, and we made room in our backseat for one of the guys to sit with us.

The roads were winding and very bumpy with constant turns going up and down the mountain sides on very narrow roadways. Most of the roads did not have standard guardrails. Aside from the occasional thoughts (well, let's be honest, it was more like frequent thoughts) of "God, I hope we don't go over the side of the cliff," the views were gorgeous. The mountains were big, not snow-capped like the Himalayas, but they were a mix of brown and green coloring from the trees.

There was a river flowing below that was sparse in some areas. At one point, the road actually crossed the rocky river and we drove through the water to cross it. There was no bridge in sight. It was literally just a bunch of rocks strategically placed so the tires could get some traction. It was very bumpy, and I noticed that I was holding my backpack tight in my lap like a baby, almost like, "see? I protected you!"

Yes, I know I'm dramatic.

At that point, our driver's playlist had shifted from straight techno music to a mix of traditional Nepali music and some upbeat songs. One particular song had my full attention. I had no idea what the words were, but it was quite catchy. The words I could pick out (or at least I thought that it was what they were saying) were "motorcycle turn it up, something, something else, Sindhuli." It was a repetitive song, but I was digging it! Since there were a lot of scooters and motorcycles on the roads in Nepal, the song seemed quite fitting.

Jet lag started to creep in, so I took my airplane pillow out of my backpack, wrapped it around my neck, and took about an hour nap.

See, I knew there was another reason why I needed my backpack with me! I hope we don't have much further to drive. My motion sickness is kicking in bad.

The guy sitting next to me was smiling at me and trying to make conversation but neither of us could understand the other.

Insert my trusty language translation app!

I had already set it to Nepali before I arrived. Being the shy person that I am, I typed the first thing that came to mind when meeting someone new and trying not to send across the wrong message as I was not romantically interested in any way.

"So, what is the name of the river down there?"

He looked at me like I was crazy. He said something out loud; the driver laughed. He told me the name of the river (supposedly). I was trying to recite it but was failing miserably, and they were still laughing.

Clearly, what I am saying must not the be name of the river. But, whatever, might as well laugh with them!

Sophie leaned over and whispered in my ear, "I think he fancies you. Maybe he's going to ask you on a date next!"

"Oh geez!" I replied as we giggled.

...

After the long six-hour drive, we arrived in Sindhuli.

Finally. I am miserably nauseous. I have a bad headache and feel weak, dizzy, and lightheaded. I just need to get something to eat. I have some fig bars in my backpack, but I really need a meal. Thanks a lot, motion sickness...you never fail to hit me at the most inopportune time.

Sophie and I got our bags off the top of the Jeep and walked toward the office where we were supposed to meet up with the other volunteers. Sophie put her rucksack on her back, slid her regular backpack on the front of her body, and walked with ease.

Meanwhile, there was me, with my heavy ass backpack—that damn laptop—and my rolling suitcase which held all the things I needed for my trip but was highly impractical for navigating the rocky Nepali streets. I was purely exhausted, and the walk was of course uphill. I swear, it seemed like the hill never ended. The wheels of my suitcase kept gathering rocks which would make it suddenly stop rolling. Sophie got further and further away.

"You alright back there?" she yelled at me when she saw how far back I was.

"I got it! I'm good!"

I am not good. I feel sick. This is the worst walk EVER. Ouch!

My suitcase wheel caught another rock, this time jolting the bag so hard that it turned over onto its side and twisted my wrist to the right awkwardly.

I want to give up. This walk sucks. Stupid suitcase with stupid wheels and stupid heavy ass laptop backpack! Ugh!

After what felt like an eternity, we made it to the office. I removed my shoes as it is customary in Nepali culture and sat down on the floor while eating a fig bar out of my backpack.

Already waiting in the office was Miranda, a lovely woman from California who had been on previous disaster response projects in Nepal. I was doing my best to be conversational, but my headache was so intense, and I still felt weak.

After about thirty minutes of nauseated hell, we received word that we would be leaving to head to the volunteer base. Other volunteers had showed up and were waiting outside; Claudia and Luis, a cute couple from Mexico who were traveling around the world, and the Giulias, two Italian women who looked so adorable together. One of the Giulias is a civil engineer specializing in seismic engineering. She was awaiting word from a job offer for the United Nations to work on a project rebuilding homes in Nepal after the earthquake.

The driver offered to take all our bags and piled them all on top of the Jeep. Seeing how my suitcase fared well on the first drive, I let the driver put my backpack up top as well.

See? Even despite being sick I was able to bring down the drama factor a notch or two.

We were told that the last drive was going to be another two and a half hours, so I politely asked (well, begged) to sit in the front seat next to the driver so that I could control my motion sickness. Everyone nicely agreed, and we got on our way.

...

The drive to Marin was even bumpier than the trip from Kathmandu because most of the roads were mainly rocks and dirt. We drove up and down the mountain sides and through small villages.

The views away from the city were different and very beautiful. There were rice paddies embedded in the mountainsides, and from far away they look like stairs that you could take up to the mountaintops. Because I was able to sit in the front seat, the drive went much better for me. I was able to rest some and get over my motion sickness.

As we entered the Marin volunteer base that was set up on a rice paddy, I saw a tool shed on the right made of silver corrugated galvanized iron (CGI). The metal was crimped and resembled waves. Straight ahead were two bright orange bunkhouses and bamboo shower stalls with blue tarp for shower curtains. To the left was a volleyball court, the staff office, and a pavilion.

We got out of the car, gathered our bags, and were introduced to some of the staff.

"Tiffany, you are in that bunk right over there."

Ahhhhhh! AWESOME! MY PRAYERS HAVE BEEN ANSWERED! THANK GOD! A BOTTOM BUNK!

I had to play it cool. "Perfect, thank you," I replied quietly.

I blew up my air mattress and retrieved my sleeping bag and blankets. I pulled out my thermals, hat, neck wrap, and headlamp so that I was ready for the evening. I decided, since I had time, to pull out my work clothes. I brought the same jeans that I wore in Puerto Rico and North Carolina.

I smiled, thinking of the previous work I did and knowing that my experience in Nepal was going to add to it. I had grown so much in my recovery since I went to Puerto Rico, and there I was, all the way across the world! I forced my bulky suitcase under the bunk bed and walked out to explore the base some more.

The volunteers were starting to come back from their workday and were introducing themselves. As hard as I was trying to be sociable, it was difficult because I'm so shy.

I just need to get comfortable, and then I'll open up and not be so nervous. There's just so many people and so many names to remember. This is hard.

At 6:00 p.m. we had our meeting in the pavilion. It was an open pavilion with picnic tables, prayer flags hanging from the ceilings, a big white board with volunteer and project information, a drinking water station, and the lost and found. At the meeting, we went over the work that was done during the day, the work that would be accomplished the next day, reviewed any news that needed to be announced to the volunteers, and did welcome/goodbye speeches.

Dear sweet baby Jesus, here we go again with the welcome speech. Please don't let me make a fool out of myself!

Did I mention that I hate public speaking? Because I really hate public speaking.

"Hi, I'm Tiffany. I'm from Virginia Beach, Virginia. This is my third All Hands and Hearts project. The two other projects I volunteered at were in Barranquitas, Puerto Rico and Bayboro, North Carolina. I'll be here for two weeks. Nice to meet you all."

My anxiety was through the roof. *Could I have been any more dull or boring?*

I had just enough signal to text my kids and e-mail my parents to let them know I arrived safely. The internet signal was very spotty and did not allow for any scrolling on Facebook. WhatsApp, Facebook Messenger, and Gmail were my lifelines to my home across the world.

We only had generator power between 5:00 p.m. and 9:00 p.m. Once 9:00 p.m. hit, the lights went out and turned into quiet hours. The temperature had dropped quickly. I dressed in a layer of thermals, wool socks, a hoodie, and my neck scarf. I tucked myself into my insulated sleeping bag by 8:30 p.m. Being so exhausted from all the traveling, I quickly fell into a deep slumber.

Of course, the ever constant middle-of-the-night-totally-inconvenient 2:30 a.m. urge to pee never fails me.

My face felt so cold and I was afraid to feel what it was like outside of my sleeping bag. I didn't have enough internet signal to use the weather app on my phone to verify what the actual temperature was, but if I had to guess, it was about twenty degrees Fahrenheit (in reality, it was probably more like upper thirties or forties, but we all know by now I'm an exaggerator).

Okay. It's freaking freezing. The last thing I want to do is get out of this sleeping bag, because I'm toasty warm in here, but my face is frozen. I don't want to wake anyone up either.

I mentally prepared myself for all the steps I was going to have to do in order to go pee:

Step 1: Very carefully, quiet as a mouse, unzip my sleeping bag while I clench my teeth.

The unzipping was actually loud as fuck. The slower I unzipped, the louder and more amplified it got. The faster I unzipped, you guessed it, the louder and more amplified it got, just with a high-pitched zippier sound.

Step 2: Ever so quietly, maneuver out of my sleeping bag.

The sleeping bag sounded like a loud rustling of leaves that just wouldn't quit. Oh! And my air mattress made a wonderfully loud groaning sound as I moved.

Step 3: Holy shit it's freezing...okay, focus. I need to find my headlamp. Where the hell is my headlamp? I KNOW I put it next to my sleeping bag.

After searching aimlessly and accidentally kicking over my metal water bottle that made a really loud echoing sound on the tile floor, I found the headlamp.

I placed the headlamp on my head, turned it on the low red light setting, and made my way to the door. I found my slip-on shoes and stepped outside into the night air.

The air was so cold but refreshing and smelled very clean. I looked up and I was in absolute awe. The sky was pitch black and clear without a single cloud. The moon was enormous, sitting among a blanket of millions of big and bright stars.

I'm high up in the mountains, in the middle of nowhere, and it almost feels like I am the only one up here. The air is still. I don't hear any animals or insects.

I stood there, staring at the sky while turning around slowly. The constellations I loved seeing as a child in the Pennsylvania mountains, like the Big Dipper and Orion's Belt, looked so much more pronounced up there. Stars were stretching beyond the horizon.

This is absolutely incredible. My childhood dream of being an astronaut doesn't seem so silly right now. I'm picturing myself flying up in those stars and seeing the Earth from space. I feel like I can reach out and grab the moon, it seems that close. I feel complete serenity. I'm actually here in Nepal. Tomorrow I'm going to help build a school. Is this all real? I have to be dreaming. And if I'm dreaming, I don't want to wake up quite yet.

After a few minutes, my bladder decided to be the one to spoil the daydream. I used the restroom and, as quietly as I could, returned to my bed.

CHAPTER SIXTEEN

BACKFILL, BUCKETS, AND BRICKS, OH MY!

———

Why is it five thousand degrees in here?
Why does literally every muscle in my body hurt?
And what the hell is that buzzing sound?

It was 5:45 a.m. The vibrations of my cell phone alarm going off next to me woke me up out of a deep sleep. I must have been really cold that night because I was completely buried in my insulated sleeping bag. I grabbed my cell phone so I could turn off the alarm. The screen was all fogged up. I wiped away the built-up condensation, turned off the alarm, and checked for an internet signal.

Dammit. No internet. I hope the kids don't think that I'm ignoring them.

I sent text messages to my kids, anyway, hoping they would go through at some point despite the nine hour and forty-five-minute time zone difference.

As soon as I pulled down the sleeping bag off my face, the cold brisk air sent a tingling sensation across my cheeks. A lot of people were still sleeping so I quietly tried to exit my sleeping bag (I wasn't so successful in the quietly part) to go eat some breakfast.

I am not the type of person who can just get up, get dressed, and go. I need time to sit, drink some tea, and collect my thoughts before I start my day. I opted to change into my work clothes in the dark while everyone slept because the darkness offered me privacy.

I strategically placed my work jeans, socks, sports bra, underwear, and purple All Hands and Hearts work shirt directly beneath my bed so that I wouldn't need to search for it. As I removed my layers of thermals that I slept in the night before, I got colder. I pulled the freezing cold and slightly damp jeans up my legs.

I didn't know it was possible to feel even colder. My love affair with tea will help me get warm!

I put on my black heavy coat, buff neck wrap, and a hat, and walked outside of the bunkhouse. I saw the shadow of one of the volunteers next to a small fire. After a breakfast of tea, bread with strawberry jam, and oatmeal with sugar and strawberry jam mixed in, I decided to sit by the fire before I headed to the work site.

This tea is incredible. Plus, I love the smell of the campfire.

Three cups of tea later, and regretting it because I already needed to pee, I walked along the bumpy dirt road from the base to the first school site, Thakureshwor. I carried my purple water bottle and purple cinch bag. In my bag there was a fig bar, an orange, sunscreen, my cell phone and portable charger, my sunglasses, and some Aleve.

I didn't forget anything, did I? Why am I so nervous? I've done these projects before. Well, not on this scope. Did I dress warm enough? I still feel so cold.

I walked past a small home and there were two baby goats jumping around playing with each other.

All those viral videos I've spent hours of my life watching that I'll never get back about baby goats playing really are so much better in person! I wonder what my Jack Russells would do if I had a baby goat running around the back yard.

It was literally the cutest thing to watch. One of the baby goats was leaping from left to right and up and down. It turned in circles and didn't have a care in the world about where in the world it ended up. The mother was drinking some water close by while keeping an eye on her babies. Chickens and roosters were pecking the ground.

A woman wearing a bright red *Kurta Suruwal*, a traditional Nepali dress, stood nearby the animals. She was squatting down on the ground while washing plates and bowls in a shallow metal basin. As I turned and started to walk up a small hill toward the building site, the cold feeling in my body faded, distracted by the sunrise ahead of me.

The small, bright yellow sun was peeking over the mountainside with orange and pink haze surrounding it. The small houses scattered throughout the mountainside rice paddies were still shadowed, yet to be awakened by the kiss of the sun's light.

What a beautiful reminder of the importance and greatness of new beginnings. Like the sun starting a new day, I'm about to have a fresh start in my life. Traveling so far away and disconnecting from technology is helping me reconnect with myself again. It's like this trip is helping me press the reset button on my life since I'm about to go through divorce again.

As I rounded another corner, I saw the four brick buildings of the Thakureshwor school that were in the early phases of construction. The short layers of brick and mortar met the numerous rebars that were stretching toward the sky, outlining how tall the layers of brick and cement would eventually be. *This is going to be a helluva lot different than the hurricane response projects. I wonder what they will have me work on?* At our morning meeting, the group of volunteers, All Hands and Hearts staff, and Nepalese male and female masons all stood in a circle. We introduced ourselves to the group by saying our names and what country we were from. There were men and women from countries all over the world including the United Kingdom, Wales, Lebanon, Ireland, the United States, Mexico, Nepal, Poland, India, Singapore, Canada, Czech Republic, Germany, Italy, Spain, France, Ecuador, and Lithuania. We also did stretches and light exercises such as jumping jacks.

There's got to be like sixty people here. This is crazy! Come on nerves, calm down. I've done projects before. Why do I always get so nervous? And damn I need to work out more. Am I seriously this winded after doing jumping jacks? Jumping jacks, the easiest exercise ever. Get it together, girl!

Rowan, the Site Coordinator, pulled out a large white board. *Ah, here we go. Time to find out what I'll be doing today.*

In big letters at the top, it said "Let's Build a School!" with categories beneath it that read: "Form Work, Backfill, Windows, Bricks, Mix & Move, Form Prep/Rebar, Cupcakes, and Rebar." Volunteer and mason names were written below each category.

Cupcakes? In construction? Whatever it is, it sounds cute.

I walked up to the board to find my name.

Please let my name be under cupcakes. Or bricks even! Just something I think I can do.

Of course, just my luck; my name wasn't under either of those. I immediately started searching each category. There it was, my name in a list of nine, including my new friends Luis and Miranda that I met in Sindhuli, under "Backfill." My eyes widened in confusion.

What in the world does backfill even mean? Does it involve heavy lifting? I sure hope not. I'm not strong at all! I guess I'll figure it out as I go. Time to find some PPE.

I was handed a yellow hard hat. I smiled because it reminded me so much of the one I wore in Puerto Rico.

This time is different though; this time it actually fits!

I made my way over to Building 1 where I was given a shovel and a backfill tamper, which is a pole with a round weighted bottom. Wheelbarrows of dirt were being dumped into the area where I was standing, which would eventually be the entrance to the building.

I spread the dirt evenly and as soon as I finished spreading one pile, another was waiting. Two guys were using plate compactors which offered an easier solution to compact the dirt versus doing it manually with the tamper.

"I'm Mike and this is Przemek. We are going to be helping you with backfill."

"Awesome, nice to meet you guys! I'm Tiffany."

"Where are you from, Tiffany?" Mike asked me.

"The US. Where are you guys from?"

Mike spoke up first. "I'm from England."

Przemek spoke next. "And I'm from Poland."

How. Freaking. Cool! I love meeting new people from around the world.

As the sun rose, I started to feel hot. I was not used to that type of manual labor and my lower back was already starting to ache. I drank a lot of water but couldn't seem to quench my thirst.

After four hours of backfilling, we walked back to the volunteer base for lunch. I learned right away that lunch everyday was dal bhat, the same dish that I had on my first night in Thamel with Sophie.

Good thing I enjoy the taste of it since it looks like there will be a ton of dal bhat in my near future. But woah! This batch is quite spicy! My stomach better not hate me later for this.

...

Time to see what this bucket shower thing is all about.

The volunteers all shared four showers made of bamboo and blue tarps as shower curtains. Depending on what time you got in line for the showers determined how long you waited. It was a "bucket shower" system, meaning I got a bucket of hot water (if it was available!) and then mixed it with the cold water that came from a spicket inside of the shower. My body was still hot from the sun and workday, but the air was starting to get cold.

Well, this is different. So primitive. I love it!

I climbed into the bamboo shower stall and removed my sweaty and dirt-covered clothing. Standing in front of my pink water bucket, I looked down into it. I took the small cup, scooped the water, and poured it over my chest. The water felt so warm and inviting. I opted to wash my hair and body as quickly and efficiently as possible so that I could enjoy the rest of the warm water until the bucket ran empty.

This is certainly the most interesting shower I have ever taken. It feels so natural out here in the remote mountains.

I found the situation funny because, prior to my trip to Puerto Rico years ago, I would have been so uncomfortable showering like that because I took the hot water and American showers that I was used to for granted. The cold showers in Puerto Rico and Nuevo Durango gave me appreciation for a shower in any capacity.

This bamboo bucket shower is definitely enhancing my experience here in Nepal.

Careful to not slip on the circular bamboo floor, I finished my shower, dried off, and put on thermals for the evening.

The sun set quickly, and the air got colder by the minute. I brushed my wet hair and pulled it back into a braid. After the evening meeting and dinner (yes, it was dal bhat!), I was exhausted from the jet lag and backfilling. I joined the other volunteers by the fire and noticed that a lot of the volunteers were smoking cigarettes.

Oh, lord, here we go. I'm not going to be able to resist this. Maybe if I have just one...

"Hey, Tony, do you have an extra cigarette?" Tony, my new friend, is a gentleman from Wales.

"Of course, beautiful bird," he responded in his unique accent.

I smiled. *Well, this is a first. I've never been called a bird before!*

By 8:25 p.m., I was bundled up and already in bed, praying for a good night's rest.

...

Why did I do this to myself again?

Five-thirty in the morning crept on me very quickly. I slept well for the most part, but my body was very achy and sore. I honestly felt a little discouraged.

Did I really sign up for two weeks of this? My body already feels defeated. Am I going to be able to handle the other type of work that they sign me up for?

I recognized that the self-doubt that crept in was something that I had battled a lot over the years. That damn self-doubt that made me believe that I wasn't worth doing anything good and that I was incapable of achievements.

Still lying in bed, I closed my eyes, took a deep breath in, and breathed out slowly.

God, grant me the serenity to accept the things I cannot change, the courage to change the things I can, and the wisdom to know the difference.

I made a deal with myself to prove myself wrong and let my confidence win. I couldn't change the physical aches and pains my body felt, but I could choose to muster up the courage to fight through the pain with confidence and determination rather than let the self-doubt win.

After a breakfast of oatmeal with strawberry jam and sugar and two cups of tea, I was in a Jeep heading toward the alternate school site, Janakalyan. It was a forty-five-minute drive down the curvy bumpy mountain roads. As we drove along, we passed children that were walking to school. The windows were rolled down, welcoming in the brisk mountain air.

The children smiled at us and pressed their little hands together in front of their chests like in a form of prayer. They yelled "Namaste!" with excitement in their voices. We reciprocated the acts from inside the car. It was so sweet and endearing to see the children and know that the school I was helping build would be theirs someday. It seemed like they were so grateful and full of joyful anticipation about their new school already.

That right there is what this experience is all about! It's not all about me, my sore muscles, and discomforts from being so far away from home. I'm helping others and learning to be more grateful for the things that I do have.

It may have been a coincidence, but suddenly my body didn't ache anymore. I was ready to take on more challenging tasks.

Once we arrived to Janakalyan, we had our morning ritual of stretches, exercises, and introductions. Janakalyan had just one school building and was adjacent to an existing school with yellow walls. Children were laughing and watching us from the balcony.

My day consisted of two hours of backfilling and then mixing masala with Charlotte, Phil, and Nick. Masala (yes, pronounced the same as tiki masala!) is a mixture of sifted sand, dry concrete, and water. We mixed it all by hand with shovels and it got quite heavy.

Well, let's be real. Literally everything is heavy to me. I already know I'm going to be even more sore from this tomorrow but it's okay. Seeing the little faces peeking over the edge of the balcony and smiling down at us makes the hard work worth it.

The sunrise during my walk on the first morning
of work at Thakureshwor, Marin, Nepal.

Thakureshwor school building site number one at the All Hands and Hearts Marin project, Nepal.

CHAPTER SEVENTEEN

A NIGHT AT THE MASON'S HOUSE

———

Shovel, water, PPE! Backfill is so fun for me!
  Positive attitude, one, two, three! Sore legs and back won't bother me!
  Spread that dirt evenly! Don't give up 'til 10:30!
Ten-thirty was important, you see, because that's when it was water, snack, and smoke break time.

I had my shovel ready at the Janakalyan school site. There was a small group of us: me, Mike, Phil, Charlotte, Luisana, Rohith, James, Nick, Alex, and Juliette. All the other volunteers were back at the Thakureshwor school.

The mountain fog was very heavy that morning, creating a lower visibility and a cold dampness in the air. The fog created a haze around the partially built school, wrapping the bricks and rebar in a sheer blanket of white.

Rain and thunderstorms were in the forecast later that day. We were all hoping and praying that the rain would hold off until after we got back to the base because if not, the roads would have been too treacherous to drive. The masons share a house together next to the school and, if we ended up having to stay, us volunteers would have to stay in the house with them overnight.

After two hours of shoveling and evenly spreading the dirt throughout the foundation of the school, we were invited to participate in a Nepali festival. The date was January 30, which was Martyr's Day. Martyr's Day is a national holiday celebrated yearly in remembrance of four martyrs, Dharma Bhakta Mathema, Gangalal Shrestha, Dashrath Chand, and Shukraraj Shastri, who were executed in 1941 for their opposition to the Rana regime. Those who died while fighting for Nepal are also remembered. The women looked lovely with their radiant makeup and beautiful red Kurta Suruwal dresses.[6]

There was a rich smell of incense in the air. Slow melodic Nepali music was playing. First, a woman placed a *tika* on my forehead. The tika, a symbol of good luck and purity, is common in Hinduism and is made from dried turmeric and grains of rice.[7] I was also given gifts of diced apples, small chocolate candies, and pieces of crunchy ramen noodles with something yellow and sweet on them.

I can't believe that this is happening! I have to learn more about this festival when I get home. I wish I could stay in Nepal longer and experience more festivals! Learning about different cultural customs around the world is what led me to my love for anthropology and now I am living it and experiencing it. Words can't describe how grateful I am to be a part of this!

I thought back to those times when people criticized my choice of studying anthropology and how I used to feel ashamed for it.

---

6   "Martyr's Day in Nepal," Nepal Tour Guide Team, Trek & Expedition (P.) LTD, accessed June 19, 2020.

7   "Culture Preservation in Nepal," Choice Humanitarian, accessed June 19, 2020.

Now that I am participating in a celebration in a remote village of Nepal, there is no room for shame. I feel proud of myself for embracing the fact that I thrive from learning something different.

Lunch was, you guessed it, dal bhat!

After lunch, I found myself in the mud brick pool with Mike. The brick pool was made from bricks and a large blue tarp. We wore rubber boots and rubber gloves and our job was to soak the mud bricks in the shallow water for fifteen minutes while rotating them halfway through in order to strengthen their integrity. After they were done soaking, we handed them to the Nepali masons who would then take them over to the building to be added to the school walls. On average, there were over one hundred bricks in the pool at a single time.

The rubber gloves did not do the best job at keeping the red murky brick water off my hands. They were constantly saturated. My fingers already had blisters from the backfilling and handling the bricks with only rubber gloves. Two of the blisters had broken open. The one on my left palm right below my middle finger looked like it was getting infected. The other blister, on my right hand where my thumb met my palm, was being rubbed raw with every brick I picked up.

Well, that doesn't look good. I hope that the discoloration is from the muddy brick water. I'm going to have to keep an eye on these. I don't have time to worry about it now though. Just fight through the discomfort.

Bending over to pick up the bricks hurt my back after repeatedly squatting for hours. It was a different kind of pain though. It was a pain worth being proud of every time I saw the masons take the bricks from the pool by wheelbarrow over to the masons who were placing the bricks and cement onto the school walls, gradually increasing their height.

"Shit! Mike! Oh my God, did I seriously just do that?"

Mike laughed at me as I yelled when I squatted down a little too far, fell into the bricks, and got my entire butt wet.

"Mike! Ahh! Ewww! Wet denim is the worst feeling ever!"

"I don't envy you one bit right now!" he replied.

I laughed along with him because it was a nice comedic relief to the never-ending rotation of bricks.

...

Storm clouds started to roll in and the wind picked up in intensity. Juliette, our site supervisor, announced in her lilting French accent that we were going to leave early to try to make it up the mountain in time before the storm hit. We frantically packed up our tools and put them away.

"Raju! Raju, stop the Jeep! Can you stop the Jeep?"

Raju, our driver, pulled over on the side of the road. Alex, a site supervisor in training, jumped out of the car. He ran behind James, Mike, and I as we climbed out of the Jeep to see what was wrong.

"What are you doing?" James asked in his strong British accent.

I am seriously loving the different accents! The diversity is incredible.

Alex stood over a long yellowish snake in the road.

"I'm going to pick it up and get it out of the road so it doesn't get hit!" Alex said while intently watching the snake. His legs were spread, and his arms were in place, ready to grab it.

"I feel like I'm in some wild animal reality show right now," I told James and Mike.

"Are you sure it's not poisonous?" James asked. I wondered the same thing as I crossed my arms nervously in anticipation.

"It's not, trust me!" Alex said with excitement in his eyes as he picked up the snake by the tail.

The snake swung its body around while lashing at his arm and hand. As soon as he grabbed its head, the snake immediately coiled around his arm and tried to bite him several times, successful in one of its attempts.

Holy shit! Should I be worried? He doesn't look worried. The other guys are getting a kick out of this. Why am I the only one worried? He actually looks really badass right now. He looks like a warrior with his rolled-up shirt sleeves, his full sleeve tattoo showing, and bandana tied around his forehead.

"You're bleeding! Oh my God, are you okay? Did that hurt?" I asked curiously.

"I'm fine! It's not poisonous, trust me. I studied herpetology in college. This stuff gets my adrenaline going," Alex stated without hesitation while looking in wonder at the snake.

Well, damn, might as well take a picture while he's still holding it!

After James, Mike, and I took pictures, Alex placed the snake out of harm's way off the road. We continued driving toward the base. About halfway through our drive, Alex's cell phone rang.

We all froze in the backseat because we knew deep down what this call meant.

"Hello? Hello? I can't hear you. Oh wait, there you are. Okay, what were you saying? Yeah. Oh wow. Okay." He hung up the phone. He sighed heavily.

Alex turned toward Raju. "Raju, turn the car around. We can't make it up the mountain. The roads are too bad because of the rain. We have to stay at the mason's house tonight."

...

Mike and I looked at each other. We knew that was going to be a possibility, but it became a reality.

Did I pack everything I needed? Let's see. I have my toothbrush, toothpaste, contact solution, contacts case, my glasses, baby wipes, and dry shampoo. I also have a change of underwear and socks, a pair of thermals to wear tonight, my passport, and some rupees. What else do I need? I have to be forgetting something!

We arrived back at the mason's house. We were shown to our sleeping area which was a room that had concrete floors, bright pink walls, and a garage door. We spread thin mattresses and blankets across the concrete. We all picked a spot to sit against the wall while we waited out the rain.

No one had ever spent the night down here before, so it was a first for everyone. We were a little nervous but were in good spirits. Luisana pulled out her phone and played "Home" by Edward Sharpe and The Magnetic Zeros. We all smiled as we listened to that song because we mutually knew without saying it out loud that that moment was going to be the first of many experiences we were going to have that night that would bond us together.

We were all covered in dirt and sweat, and we didn't care. We were just happy to be together.

...

Let's play trivia!

What did I have for dinner?

Drum roll, please!

If you guessed dal bhat, you are correct!

But it wasn't just any ordinary dal bhat. The dal bhat that night had some different vegetables like green beans and some other type of bean mixed in and it tasted heavenly. It still had a very spicy kick to it, but the flavor was incredible. As we all sat together and ate, we laughed and joked with each other. Despite being away from base and having basically only the dirty work clothes on our backs, we had everything we needed right then and there. We had each other.

Alex and I decided to browse through the little store next to the tiny restaurant where we ate dinner. On the shelf, in a little yellow can, was a drink called "Badam Drink" with "Real Bits of Badam and Saffron."

"What do you think it tastes like?" I asked Alex as I picked up the can and looked at it.

"I have absolutely no idea. Shall we buy some and try it?"

"Yes! I'm all about trying new things."

We purchased the drinks, said a quick "Cheers!" and clicked our tiny cans of Badam Drink together.

We couldn't quite think of what to make of the taste. Our faces twisted in confusion.

"It's a lot chunkier than I expected," Alex said.

"It's not bad though!" I said as I swallowed it down.

The drink had a sweetened condensed milky flavor with bits and inconsistently sized chunks of badam (whatever that is) and saffron. All I knew was that I had to have more before I left Nepal.

After some time around a fire outside of the restaurant and store, we settled into our garage bedroom. We left the garage door slightly ajar so it would allow some air flow but still keep wild animals out.

On the right side, in order from the back, was Luisana, me, James, Alex, and Nick. On the left side was Juliette, Mike, and Phil. Charlotte and Rohith got lucky and were sleeping on the two vacant bunk beds in the house.

I'm extremely close to the back wall of the room. It's not even bothering me that I'm sleeping on the floor with these guys. They are my friends and I trust them. And a pillow! That's what I forgot. Something to use for a pillow.

The concrete floor was cold and hard. I had a hard time getting comfortable because my hip bones were digging into the floor if I laid on my side or stomach. The only comfortable position I could somewhat find was on my back. Thankfully, Nick let me borrow his coat to use as a pillow which was sweet of him.

As soon as I laid down and we turned the lights out at 9:00 p.m., I had to pee. Even though I had just gone at 8:52 p.m. By 1:00 a.m., I REALLY had to pee. I waited as long as I possibly could because I was so scared that I was going to step on someone when trying to get across the garage.

Not only do I have to successfully walk across a sea of blankets without stepping on someone, I have to then limbo under the garage door because if I try to open it more it will be incredibly loud. This is insanely nerve-wracking.

I turned my headlamp on to the red setting and tried to make out where everyone's legs were.

Okay, that blanket mound there is James' legs. Alex's aren't that close to his luckily, and Nick's are positioned so that I can quickly hop across them without stepping on them.

I skillfully made it across them. The door was only open maybe a foot and a half off the ground. I crouched down as low as I could and slid out underneath the door.

I feel like a badass ninja!

I got to the bathroom quickly and climbed back under the door. I stealthily hopped back over everyone, making sure to act extra ninja-y with the hand motions and everything. I crawled back under the covers that I shared with James and Luisana. I turned onto my right side, facing Luisana, so that I could put my glasses and headlamp back up against the wall.

At that exact moment, James rolled over, and his back was right against mine.

I can't roll back over now, otherwise I'll wake him. But hey, he's making it more comfortable.

I smiled because the experience of a night spent with a small group of volunteers away from the base was so unique and different. Who gets to say they spent a night in a mason's house in a remote village in Nepal? Not many people can! We literally weathered the storm together.

That night, hands down, had been one of the best nights of my life. I'll never forget it.

I made myself comfortable with James against my back. His body heat provided warmth, something I welcomed against the cold concrete floor.

The next morning, it was back to backfilling. I was still sore and achy from sleeping on the concrete floor and backfilling once again added to that pain. I was trying my best to keep up with the piles of dirt that were getting poured into my section, but I felt sluggish and weak.

James called out to me from across the trench we were working in. "Hey Tiffany, can you help me over here?"

I walked slowly over to him with my shovel while breathing heavily. "Sure, what's up?"

"Can you spread this dirt out for me? You are so much better at it than I am. You actually do it perfect. I don't know how you get it so even but the way you do it makes the compacting really even. Do you mind?"

Oh wow. Wait, what? Is he serious? Me? Perfect at spreading dirt?

"Sure thing, no problem!" I told him, thankful for his kind words and appreciation. It was amazing what a simple compliment did for me.

I remember when I was depressed and thought that none of my actions deserved any praise. When I did get praise, and Alex did praise me often, I didn't believe the words to be true. As my confidence and self-esteem grew over time through volunteering, traveling, challenging myself, and meeting new people, I learned to accept compliments and use them to motivate me and drive me further.

James' words gave me a boost of energy that made me want to keep pushing and exerting myself even more. My back didn't ache so much, and I felt peppier in my step.

Rohith and I playing shovel guitars...I mean sifting sand to prepare for the masala, or concrete, at the Janakalyan school site, Nepal.

We all got broken sleep. We were all quite tired, but the morale and spirits were so high because we had that bonding time together. We shared a one-of-a-kind experience and we all felt connected in a way that went further than just new friendships. We were a family.

We played music and sang together while we worked.

The kids were peeking over the balcony of the school. They were always curious about what we were working on. They giggled and laughed at us and it was so exhilarating to know that the work we were doing was going to benefit them someday.

The heartwarming community of volunteers, my new family in my "home away from home," were so supportive and encouraging. It made being away from my real home a tiny bit easier.

I pushed through the pain knowing that the work not only strengthened my body, but it also strengthened my mind and soul.

CHAPTER EIGHTEEN

THERAPY ON A NEPALESE MOUNTAIN

———

Why, for the life of me, can't I ever sleep in? Like ever?

I could stay up until 3:00 a.m. I can be so freaking tired that I can't function. But no matter what, I will be wide awake no later than 7:00 a.m. without fail.

So annoying.

Ugh.

Since our volunteer workdays ran Sunday through Friday, Saturdays were our only days off. I was looking forward to sleeping in a little bit, but being the early bird that I am, I was wide awake by 6:30 a.m. I made my third cup of tea and sat down on a piece of damp plywood next to the fire. I lit up my cigarette and placed it between my index and middle fingers while I held the small teacup in my hand. I held my hands out in front of me, welcoming the warmth of the flames from the fire near my skin.

I was content sitting in that spot all morning while drinking tea and smoking cigarettes. It was nice to just listen to the other volunteers talk about how they were going to spend their days off. Some were talking about going to a carnival down at the bottom of the mountain. Others were opting for a quiet day on base or a hike.

I frequently, but casually, glanced over toward the bunkhouses looking for Rohith, wondering when he was going to wake up. Rohith was a young but mature guy in his early twenties from India who taught English to elementary age children.

He carried himself very well and was the epitome of tall, dark, and handsome with his thick black hair and beard. We made plans to take a hike down to the river.

I've had five cups of tea. I know I'm going to regret drinking this much once we start hiking but it tastes so good! Ah, there he is!

Rohith waved as he was walking toward me. "Ready to go to the river?"

"As ready as I'll ever be!" I replied.

We set off on the dirt road that winded through the mountains and tried to make our way downhill to the river. Not even ten minutes into the walk, I already had to pee.

Dammit. How long have we been walking? I looked at the time on my phone. *We've only been walking for ten minutes? Of course. Of freaking course.*

As we walked, there were times of silence and times of typical get-to-know-you type questions, like how long we were volunteering there for (he was signed up for seven weeks) and what we would be doing after our volunteer time was done (he had plans to travel to Pokhara for a trek).

After walking downhill for about an hour, and already knowing I was going to dread the hike back uphill, our path came across what looked like a river. There were huge boulders that stretched from the right as far as we could see up the mountain. To our left, a path of boulders climbed down the mountainside. There was a small pool of water to the right of our path that was nestled into the boulders with tiny minnows swimming throughout the clear water.

"Is this…it?" Rohith asked hesitantly.

"I don't know, I mean it has to be. It looks like it was a river at some point or will be at some point…" I replied.

"During the next monsoon!" we said at the same time. We laughed and gave each other high fives along with one of those hey-we-said-that-at-the-same-time looks.

I HAVE TO PEE.

Three other volunteers, Mike, Natasha, and Haley, had hiked separately from us and joined Rohith and I at the river pool. I ventured off up the boulder trail and found a spot where nobody would be able to see me.

That relief was the best feeling ever, let me tell you!

Rohith and I found two big boulders that were separate but close in proximity to lay down on. We closed our eyes and rested there for about a half hour.

I'm soaking in the smell of the mountain air. It's so quiet and serene. I just want to embrace this tranquility for a while. It's nice to just be able to relax and not have to physically exert myself.

We were silently enjoying each other's company, which was so comforting.

Our walk back up the mountain was definitely not as easy as the walk down. At a little over the halfway point, there was a beautiful spot to sit and overlook the valley. We sat down beside each other on the grass.

The best way I can describe the friendship I had with Rohith is that there are some people you come across in life who have such a positive energy about them. His presence was naturally comforting. There was something special about Rohith. I felt protected by him in a way because although I was enjoying my time there, I still felt somewhat alone emotionally.

"Do you have any smokes on you?" he asked me after a while.

"I have one left. Do you want to share it with me?" I replied.

"Yes, let's totally share it!" he said.

We sat in silence together and passed the cigarette back and forth while looking over the mountains and valley. The view was breathtaking. The brown rice paddies were more pronounced out there. It looked like there were little stairways embedded into all the greenness of the mountains surrounding us. The skies were overcast. The temperature was perfect; not too hot and not too cool.

It was peaceful and tranquil—a welcomed change from the busyness of the work sites and active base life. For those moments, it felt like Rohith and I were the only ones there for miles and miles. I had no idea what he was thinking about, but I respected his privacy and didn't pry.

I actually used the time to do some soul searching.

I've been in Nepal for almost a week. I came here hoping to find some peace of mind with a decision about how to proceed with my life. What is it that I really want in life? For the first time, I think the answer is clear to me. I want to feel emotionally safe. No, I need to feel safe in order to stay emotionally strong. If I don't feel safe, I will quickly go back down the rabbit hole of depression. I can't risk that anymore. I refuse to go back there.

Tears started to slowly fall down my cheeks.

I've come too far, and I've achieved so much. I'm proud of myself. I actually love myself again. I'm the most confident that I've felt in a long time. I can't stay in my marriage. I love Alex, I really do, but we have just grown so distant and we barely know each other anymore. We aren't bad people. We just aren't right for each other. I don't want to hurt him or the kids. I just want peace. I'm ready to move forward with my life. I'm just so fucking scared to start over.

The groan of a neighboring bull broke the silence. Rohith looked over at me and saw my tears. He scooted closer to me and put his arm around me, pulling my head to his shoulder. I let the tears fall for a minute or two more.

"You're going to make it through this. You're going to be okay," Rohith whispered.

"I know. I'm just scared."

"C'mon, let's start walking back to base and get lunch."

"Totally. I'm starving."

"Want to listen to music while we walk? Your choice."

"Have you heard of the Avett Brothers?"

"No, play me something good by them."

"Well, geez, way to make it difficult for me to pick the first one. They have so many great songs!"

I pulled up my Spotify playlist, put on "Live and Die" and we started walking back up the mountain.

"Hey, this is really good! I like it!" Rohith said.

I squealed in delight. "See? I told you! They are amazing!"

"I'm going to have to listen to more of their music for sure. Send me your playlist."

See, Avett Brothers? Now you have a new fan that will be listening across the world in India! You're welcome!

...

"Tiffany! Tiffany!" A group of girls in their blue school uniforms ranging from toddler age to teenagers were calling me over to the fence. I smiled and walked over to them.

"Namaste!" I said as I held my hands up to my chest in prayer position. I took off my hard hat and work gloves. The girls reached out to give me hugs, high fives, and handshakes.

A little girl, probably no older than nine years old, smiled at me as she placed a beautiful red flower behind my ear.

I was in tears. *What a sweet and kind gesture! She picked this flower just for me? What an incredible gift.*

"*Dhanyavad!*" I thanked her in Nepalese and gave her a hug.

The children were learning English and were eager to practice their new knowledge on me. They asked me simple phrases like "How are you?," "How old are you?," "Where do you work?," and "Do you have children?"

I eagerly answered their questions.

"You are beautiful, very beautiful," one of the teenage girls, who looked about fourteen years old, told me with a big smile.

"Thank you! You are beautiful, too! You are all very beautiful!" I replied, looking at all the girls while giving them high fives.

"Do you have picture of children?" she asked me.

"Yes, I do!" I pulled out my phone and pulled up a picture of Elora, Dylan, and Mason.

She pointed at Dylan. "Ohhhh, is that your son?" she asked with a huge smile and blushing cheeks.

"Yes, he is! His name is Dylan and he is thirteen."

"Your son, Dylan, is very beautiful. So beautiful!"

This is so cute. So so cute! Little does Dylan know that he has some admirers all the way across the world!

I laughed. "Do you want to see more pictures of Dylan?"

"Yes, more pictures of beautiful Dylan," she said excitedly. Her friends were now grinning from ear to ear too.

This little bonding moment between me and the girls was so special because I enjoy interacting with members of the community. I love feeling involved and one with the culture of the people I am helping.

I can't wait for the school to be finished so that all the children can enjoy this. I am going to miss their little smiling faces so much!

...

Have you heard of the famous saying "time flies when you're working your ass off on a disaster response project?"

Well, I can assure you, it's quite true!

My days during my second week in Nepal flew by quickly. I spent the remaining days working at the Thakureshwor school site doing formwork, which was assisting in bending and cutting rebar. Oh! And I finally made the "Cupcake" list! The cupcakes are little cement circles that hold the rebar in place.

I noticed that the closer it got to going home, the more nervous I felt. I found that I was often trying to retreat at lunchtime to a secluded place to cry and reflect for a few minutes.

I'm just scared of the process of divorce again. I hate tension and I don't want any animosity. Since I left for this trip, Alex and I have been getting along well through text messages. But despite that, I just don't feel connected to him anymore.

What's going to happen when I get home? Will he move out right away? Are we going to argue and fight? What is my life going to look like? Am I going to be financially stable? Am I going to be able to travel on a trip like this again? It's all a little scary and overwhelming. How am I going to break this news to my kids? I don't want to hurt anyone. I don't want to ruin anyone's life. I don't want to disappoint anyone or let anybody down, but at the same time I have to take care of myself.

I pulled the flower that the little girl gave me out of my cinch bag. As I sat alone, I held up the flower as I looked down the hill at the temporary school and watched the kids run around and play.

I'm emotionally tired but also feeling healed at the same time. It's a strange but welcomed sensation.

I felt healed because sitting there at the top of the mountain overlooking the wide valley, being there in that tiny village in a beautiful country across the world, surrounded by the welcoming locals and generous volunteers, not only helped me reach an important life decision but also provided room for my heart to grow bigger.

Tears were still falling.

I can't believe I was so scared to come here at first. I'm glad I didn't let the self-doubt creep in last week when I was so tired and my body was the most sore it has ever been. Listen to their little laughs as they chase each other around. Look at those smiles! The kids are so excited for their new school. Gosh, they are proving to the world that the little simple things in life are what matters most. I just feel so...happy.

I gained a source of strength from those children and my fellow volunteers that I was going to carry with me for the rest of my life. That was the priceless gift I received in Nepal.

This is the view from the Thakureshwor building
site where I would sit and reflect on life.

...

Later that evening after dinner (dal bhat!), a majority of volunteers were hanging out around the campfire, talking and listening to music from genres across the board. The freeing part about that was the lack of internet signal. We were all enjoying each other's company, interacting with one another, and getting to know each other on a deeper level.

I sat next to Rohith and quietly observed everyone while I drank my tea. It was a refreshing feeling to just sit back and listen to all the stories of people traveling, their adventures, and all the different places they have been.

I started to feel envious of their ability to just not have a plan and be okay with that.

I grew up fast so young due to having children at an early age. I kind of feel like life has quickly passed me by and there is so much of the world that I haven't seen yet. I love being a mom though. I wouldn't trade those moments for anything. It's crazy that I saved up all my vacation days for the year at work just to come here. Some people have been here for a couple months and they are going to travel somewhere else next.

How does it feel to be that carefree? How does it feel to not have a plan? Well, that's all a daydream for me right now. I'm about to be a single mom again. I can't travel on that sort of level anytime soon. And...that's okay. I'll get my chance someday.

I probably looked funny to everyone else because I'm not able to hide my facial expressions. I was lost in a daze. I held my empty teacup up to my chest, entranced by the orange and red flames of the fire flickering in the darkness.

There were small groups of people talking among themselves around the fire. Charlotte, or Bobby, as the Nepali children called her because they couldn't pronounce her name, talked about her adventures in Sri Lanka. Sonja, with her eccentric and amazing sense of style that I wish I could pull off, was laughing and joking around with Natasha. Sonja's laugh was contagious. I couldn't help but smile if I heard her laughing.

Claudia and Luis, the couple from Mexico that I met in Sindhuli, had plans to travel to Vietnam for three months after leaving Nepal. Sophie was about to take on the Everest base camp trek next. Kayla was heading to the Philippines to volunteer on another All Hands and Hearts project. Sinead opted for a yoga retreat in Bali, Indonesia.

The crackling sound of the embers was so soothing. As I stared into the fire, I disappeared into my thoughts once again.

If I had the ability to buy a one-way ticket here, how long would I have stayed in Nepal? Where would I go next? The world is so vast; how can I choose? How much money would I need to bring with me to provide food and shelter for myself for that long?

I have some destinations on my bucket list, like traveling to see Inca ruins in Peru and Italy to see Pompeii—places that will feed my desire to learn culture and history. I love the inner anthropologist within me. I really want to volunteer at an orphanage in Africa or at a refugee camp.

I smiled because I didn't view those thoughts as "Oh, I would like to do that someday, but I probably never will." I thought of those destinations as goals. That determination brought even more warmth to my soul.

Does the thought of traveling with one-way tickets from here to there frighten me? Absolutely. In fact, the thought scares the shit out of me, because of the fear of the unknown. But that's what makes this even more freeing and exciting. I'm

*inviting a sense of adrenaline into my soul and veins now
that years ago I would have thought I was incapable of feeling,
instead entangling myself with emotions of doubts, insecurity
and inability. I am growing stronger in myself in this moment.*

*I aspire to be a storyteller, a woman who shares her enter-
taining and impactful travel stories with others so that they
can be inspired and motivated to pursue new adventures.*

I heard cheering and celebration behind me. I turned
around and looked up. Miranda, the base resident champion
of ping pong, had just defeated another volunteer by a land-
slide. Their laughter made me smile even more.

I leaned my head on Rohith's shoulder. He countered by
leaning his head on mine.

"Wanna share a smoke?" he asked.

Without hesitation, I pulled my pack of cigarettes out
of my pocket, lit one up, inhaled, and passed it over to him.

CHAPTER NINETEEN

A LIFE WORTH LIVING

———

I feel like I'm going to throw up.

"Ma'am, would you like to join us for dinner?" the sweet flight attendant asked me with her bright smile.

"Um, no, thank you," I replied while fighting back the urge to vomit.

The smells of the rich Middle Eastern foods that I loved so much on my flights to Nepal were slowly torturing me. There was a stomach bug going around the volunteer base the last couple days that I was there, and I was sure that I was in the clear from getting it.

Apparently, I was wrong.

I looked out the window, praying to see some sort of daylight that would indicate that we would be landing in New York soon. However, the night sky was ever prevalent with no sign of a sunrise in sight.

I can't remember the last time I had a headache this bad. Why is my body so achy? I don't feel hot but my God this nausea is debilitating. What time is it, anyway?

I looked at the flight tracker that was on the screen on the back of the seat in front of me.

No, how can that be? Seven more hours to go? How am I going to make it? I am so tired and everything hurts.

I gradually felt worse minute by minute.

I tried to find comfortable positions so that I could get a little bit of rest but was unsuccessful. The only position that felt somewhat comfortable involved me contorting my body with my head in between the seat and the window with my makeshift blanket pillow. However, my right side would inevitably go numb after a few minutes.

I'm never going to get any sleep. This sucks. I want to cry.

That flight was horrible compared to the previous one. My first flight from Kathmandu to Doha was pretty smooth because I still felt like a functioning human being and was able to binge-watch the rest of season two of *You* on Netflix.

Which, by the way, was so shocking and pure television gold.

...

After an incredibly painstaking seven hours of tossing, turning, and trips to the bathroom, our plane landed in New York City at 7:30 a.m. I was relieved but still struggling physically. The nausea was intense. I felt so sick and incredibly weak. I hadn't slept in over forty hours at that point and I had an eight-hour layover ahead of me.

What is wrong with me? I can't even lift my backpack. Stupid laptop, it feels like it weighs four hundred pounds! I am exhausted. How am I going to get through this layover?

With tears in my eyes, it took every bit of energy I could muster just to carry my backpack through the airport.

After I made it through the painstaking process of getting through customs, I finally found a quiet corner at a departure gate that didn't have any passengers waiting for a flight.

Please let there be a bathroom close by just in case I get really sick.

I winced in pain as I looked down the concourse. I spotted a women's restroom that wasn't too far out of reach. I slowly walked over to a vacant corner of the departure gate, placed my backpack on the floor, and slumped down. I felt a piercing pain in my lower stomach. Tears started to flow stronger as I laid in fetal position.

Please God, please stop this pain. I can't even move. I need to rest. Please.

I needed water. I tried to stand up, but my body shook from weakness. I picked up my backpack and immediately dropped it. It was just too heavy.

What's wrong with me? Do I have this coronavirus thing that I keep hearing about on the news?

At that point, the outbreak in China was really bad and there were just a few cases in Washington state. I clenched my teeth as I gathered all the strength I had to pick up my backpack.

I walked slowly toward a convenience store. My vision was blurry. I bought some water and fought the pain of swallowing an Imodium that I brought in my little Ziploc bag of over-the-counter "just in case of emergency" medications.

I just want to go home.

Seven hours of laying on the airport floor, a bottle of water, two cups of tea, and a bowl of chicken noodle soup later, it was finally 3:00 p.m.

Time to board my last flight to Norfolk. FINALLY.

After the soup, Imodium, and water, I started to feel a tiny bit of relief. Since it was only going to be a one-hour flight, I felt a little surge of adrenaline that gave me enough strength to walk to my gate and board the plane. As soon as my head hit the head rest, I drifted off to sleep for the first time in nearly two days.

...

"Ladies and gentlemen, we are beginning our descent into Norfolk. We should be on the ground in about twenty minutes or so."

As I looked out the plane window, I saw the landscape, the buildings, and the Atlantic Ocean grow bigger as we got closer to land.

I'm going to be home soon. I can't wait to hug and kiss my kids. It's almost time to start my new life.

I put my earbuds in and hit shuffle on my "Reflect" Spotify playlist, which had all instrumental music. As soon as I heard the first seconds of the first song, I slightly giggled and smiled.

"Gandalf, the Wizard."

This song could not have come on at a more perfect time. I turned up the volume and closed my eyes. That time, the emotional experience was much different from the time I listened to it back in 2014.

I thought back to that time years ago. I cried so hard while looking out that car window in despair and hopelessness. I was mourning the youthful and talented girl that I used to be. I was broken and fearful, living in a constant state of anxiety, sadness, and paranoia. Death seemed like the only way to release myself from the agony.

When I looked back at who I was, it was hard for me to identify with that woman. But then again, there was a part of her that remained. Anxiety and triggers that bring on the fear of abandonment still linger, but the lived experiences I have now are constant reminders to stay strong and push through, or else that darker side could come back.

I continued to listen to "Gandalf, the Wizard" with my eyes closed. I smiled as I swayed my wrists and hands up and down and left and right, like I was conducting the music. Tears formed in my eyes, yes, but they were happy tears. Happy tears because I could feel that the lost girl I was, and my true identity, had been renewed and restored into a stronger, wiser, more joyful, and confident version of myself.

There are certain times throughout our lives when we encounter something or someone that leaves a beautiful and positive mark on our souls because of how powerful and awe-inspiring the experience was. Experiences that leave us feeling an immeasurable amount of happiness, joy, serenity, and pride can create such vivid memories that become etched into our minds. When something sparks that memory, the senses become awakened and place us right back into that period of time. It truly is such a beautiful thing.

Hearing that song made me so happy because I finally identified with the confident girl I was back in high school for the first time in a very long time. I felt full of life, full of purpose, proud of my achievements, and unaware of what lied ahead in life yet embraced being able to live in the moment.

...

What got me to this confident and beautiful place?

I pushed myself out of my comfort zone.

Did I feel silly when I was asked to make up a song and sing while playing my guitar? Yes, but when I let my inhibition go and let my voice ring freely, I felt less self-conscious and started to enjoy feeling brave. Did I feel frightened when I decided to travel to Puerto Rico to do concrete roof repair? Absolutely, but experiencing how it felt to help with disaster relief, Israel's gratitude, and learning new skills helped me figure out what I wanted to be when I "grew up." I gained motivation to start my master's program in Human Security and Resilience.

How nervous was I to take on a leadership role with AID-NOW? Incredibly nervous! But having that role and level of responsibility showed me that I am capable of being a leader. I also learned that I have it in me to delegate time to work hard as a volunteer to help the homeless children in Virginia Beach, the village of Nuevo Durango in Mexico, and the numerous other community projects we do. It's amazing to see how I naturally find the time to help a cause that I truly believe in.

How nerve-wracking was it to act out injuries during a tornado drill? I don't even know where to begin to explain how afraid, embarrassed, and intimidated I felt. I had no idea that I was going to have to act but when I succeeded, I felt exhilarated. I found myself excited for future tornado drill acting roles. However, you won't find me trying out for the lead actress role in the local theater or anything like that. I do know my limits!

How hesitant was I to use the Sawzall in North Carolina? Extremely! Power tools were intimidating to a girl who could barely use a power drill. Learning how to use new tools and subsequently help a family whose home was infested with mold helped me feel proud of myself for taking risks and trying something new.

Was I apprehensive when I realized I had to drive alone in Mexico? Of course! On the trip where it seemed like everything was going wrong, I had to keep myself from getting discouraged. When I decided to laugh at the little deviations in the plans and take things in stride, I gained a whole new perspective on staying focused, not being so nervous, and enjoying the crazy wild ride of the trip and life in general. Look at the fun story I got to tell as a result of all that chaos!

And how downright scared was I when I decided to travel across the world to Nepal? I was literally terrified! That adventure helped heal me in ways that I didn't know were possible. The jet lag and all the backfilling took a physical toll on my body that I felt at times I couldn't overcome. I was even discouraged on my first day waking up at the volunteer base because I felt self-doubt creep in.

But when I pushed myself to keep trying, to keep working through the pain, I was able to fully experience the joy and gratitude that the children showed us. Building community with and learning about life from the wonderful volunteers who have the biggest hearts (and I say that for all the volunteer projects I've worked on) has helped me grow emotionally stronger as well. That community of volunteers helped me feel valued and supported. I felt like I had a safe space to self-reflect and explore some difficult emotions.

I allowed myself to approach life with an open mind. I discovered the beauty beyond the threshold.

Let me tell you, it was so freeing and life changing. I didn't discover who I truly was until I took those steps and faced my fears. Each step made me stronger. I stopped feeling so afraid.

There's a natural high that I get from volunteering. When I take my pain and turn it into something positive, it awakens my soul. It makes me feel alive. There's something very therapeutic about pushing myself mentally and physically. Over time, I used my newfound strength and confidence to work through my emotional triggers as they tested me.

And how was I able to overcome the heartaches of another marriage ending and my son going to live with his dad? Well, I'll be honest. Those heartaches are still there. Time is slowly healing those pains.

Being a mom to three amazing children is literally the best feeling in the world. Seeing Dylan content and thriving while living with his dad and stepmom makes me feel happy for him. He is in a great music program at his high school and has made a lot of friends. Elora is a marvelous artist and is aiming to study animation in college next year. Mason, being a tween, never fails to make me laugh with all his goofy antics. While it is sad and hard to believe that Alex and I will be closing the chapter on our marriage, it's comforting to know that we still care deeply and have respect for one another.

What else has helped me heal? Forgiveness. Once I forgave myself for my transgressions and for the things that I did that not only hurt myself but hurt others as well, it opened my heart to be able to love myself again and also to forgive those who have wronged me.

It feels so freeing to not have those resentments weighing me down anymore or crippling me.

I remember when I used to place so much trust in the things I feared. My unrelenting belief in fear only made my anxiety worse. There is a phrase Alex told me years ago, but I never listened and never believed it would work. He told me, "Never trust in fear. Instead, trust in love." I didn't realize back then how powerful and true that statement was. I didn't want to see it and I couldn't believe it. But now? I'm so grateful I learned how to let go, let God handle the trials, and trust in loving myself first and foremost.

...

As the plane arrived at the gate, I began to gather my belongings. I didn't feel as sick and my backpack didn't feel as heavy as it did before. I didn't know what to expect when I walked off that plane. All I knew was that I was headed in an uncertain and scary direction, one that would impact many lives in a difficult way. I had to face it all with my head held high.

I can't wait to hug Elora, Dylan, and Mason. I'm ready to go back to work, finish up my last few classes and graduate with my Master's, prepare for the upcoming school restoration project in Mexico, and essentially start my life over again.

I was nervous but I smiled when I realized how much I'd grown. I found the happiness within myself again that I thought I had lost forever.

I have purpose now. I am so grateful to feel within every fiber of my body that I truly do have a life worth living.

I can't wait to see what lessons I'll learn and what growth I'll make during my future travels and volunteer experiences. Where in the world will I travel to next?

I stepped out of the airplane door. I took a deep breath in, exhaled, and smiled.

Everything is going to be okay.

AFTERWORD

—

I started writing this book right after my return from volunteering in Nepal. The COVID-19 pandemic was making its way across the world and my life was all of a sudden uprooted with divorce proceedings and virtual learning, all while still working full-time, going to graduate school, and well, writing. I can't tell you how many times I thought to myself, "Tiffany, you took on way too much. You aren't even a creative writer! What on earth possessed you to write a book in the first place? Nobody is going to want to read any of this!"

That self-doubt, the same self-doubt that you saw me handle throughout the book, still crept in.

I wanted to give up. If you ask my Developmental Editor, Rob, he could tell you that there were several times that I complained to him about my writing not being strong enough, that I didn't have a story worth telling, and that if I did finish the book, nobody would want to read it.

His response every time was this: "Tiffany, you are fearing rejection. Push through it. You are a writer, and what you are writing is going to help people someday. Isn't that what your book is about? Pushing through those fears and stepping out of your comfort zone? Hmm?"

Dammit, Rob. I couldn't deny the fact that he was right.

You see, in writing this book, I had to take my own advice. This process, by far, was the hardest comfort zone threshold to cross. Let me tell you though, I am so glad I did it. I learned so much about myself and in the process helped inspire readers to make positive changes in their lives.

Hearing from the readers about how my book helped them never fails to bring tears to my eyes. I've had some of the best conversations with family, friends, and complete strangers simply from sharing stories about how we've bettered ourselves from trying something new.

In the end, if all I do is help inspire one person to find strength within themselves by sharing my story, then all the hard work will have been well worth it.

Everyone's comfort zone is different, and that is what is so beautiful about the concept of this book. Sure, traveling solo and volunteering helped build my confidence and self-esteem. However, those things may not work for you, and that's okay! That's what makes this world so diverse and beautiful.

I challenge you to discover what it is that lies outside of your comfort zone. Take a step and explore it even if it's a little bit intimidating or scary. I would love to hear your story about how trying something new helped you in your path of self-discovery! You can send me an e-mail at tmosher.author@gmail.com. Let's get a conversation going!

Now, raise your cup of hot tea, and cheers to finding more beauty beyond the threshold!

ACKNOWLEDGEMENTS

Before I begin, let me first say thank you to the countless cups of hot tea and my "Reflect" Spotify playlist. The words always seemed to flow easier when I had the combination of you two around while I was writing.

And yes, that means I have a cup of hot tea close by and my music playing right now as I write this!

First and foremost, thank you to my children for your patience, for your laughter, for giving me the best gift in life of being a mother, and for finding the right time to poke fun at me during this writing process (especially when I was trying to think of the book title!). I love you all so much. To their dads, thank you to both of you for the wonderful times we did get to share together in life so that I was given the opportunity to be a mother to these three incredible children. I am so blessed.

To Mom and Dad, thank you for always being there for me and for supporting me through all my wild adventures. I know I've lived my life a little differently and did things a little out of order, yet you are still so proud of me. I wouldn't be where I am today if it wasn't for your unconditional love.

To the woman who introduced me to the Avett Brothers, Serena! Thank you for always keeping me on my toes and for never failing to point out when I'm being a huge dork. I can't wait to catch more concerts with you. You always make me laugh and I wouldn't want to share the title of sister with anyone but you. Semper Fi!

To my stepparents, Grammy, Dan, aunts, uncles, cousins, and stepsiblings, thank you for your constant love and support. I am so grateful to have you all as my family.

To Pop-Pop, Mammaw, Pampaw, and Steve, I can sense your presence daily and I know you are up in heaven feeling proud and smiling at me regarding in how far I've come. I will always carry you in my heart. I miss you more than you know.

To Kristie, thank you for being my best friend and soul sister for our entire lives. I can always count on you to make me smile, laugh hysterically, and to be a shoulder for me to lean on when I need it most. You have been through every step of life with me. Nobody knows me better than you do. I love you doll!

To Crystal, my other soul sister and fellow goddess, thank you for friendship, guidance, and love all the way from CDMX. It is a blessing that such an amazing friendship and sisterhood would blossom from volunteering together in an indigenous Mayan village in Mexico. I'll always continue to look forward to our daily chats and to see what the cards and runes have in store for me!

To All Hands and Hearts, Dreams for Mayan Children, Positive Legacy, and the Chesapeake Emergency Response Team, thank you for allowing me the opportunities to volunteer with your organizations. To the amazing volunteers I have had the pleasure of serving with, I learned so much about myself through all your wonderful hearts and souls. The impact you have on individuals and communities around the globe truly makes this world a much better place.

To Jessie, Ann, Gina, Terri, Maria, and Aaron, thank you for welcoming me to the board of AIDNOW. It is truly an honor and privilege to serve the community with a group of individuals who have the biggest hearts out of everyone I know. I can't wait to see what the future holds in store. Let's help change the world together!

To Tim, Dan, Jennifer, Phil, and the rest of the 79/84/87 crew, thank you for your endless therapy sessions and for listening to me bitch and complain whenever I felt overwhelmed with life, graduate school, writing, or a combination of the three. You all had a way of making me laugh, encouraging me, motivating me, and constantly distracting me. You rank high on the list of the best and supportive coworkers a woman could ever ask for. I'll start up donut Fridays again soon, I promise.

To my fellow authors Dmitriy, Nick, Priyanka, Mary, Nicole, Deanna, and Phillip, thank you for your texts, calls, and endless words of encouragement. I could not have asked for a better group of people to be on this incredible writing journey with.

To Eric Koester, I never imagined that a random DM on LinkedIn asking me if I want to write a book would have led to me becoming a published author nearly a year later. Thank you for listening to my half-assed pitch about what I could possibly write a book about and believing that I could turn it into something great.

To Brian Bies, thank you for your motivation, encouragement, and for giving me the chance as a first-time author to publish and share my story with the world.

To my Developmental Editor, Rob Alston, thank you for not giving up on me. I was not a creative writer when I first started working with you. I wanted to give up on the book early on. Still, you gently pushed and guided me along. I begrudgingly kept writing and over time, I learned to love it. And now, because of you, I was able to find that inner creative writer that I never knew existed and showcase her to the world. "Keep Calm and Avett On!"

To my Marketing and Revisions Editor, Kendra Kadam, thank you for helping me improve my rough first draft manuscript by asking me the most thought-provoking questions to draw out my quirkiness and deep emotions that made my book ten times better. I wouldn't have given my book that extra spiciness of my personality if it wasn't for you!

Thank you, God, for sending me all the messages and signs throughout my life in the way that you knew would make the best impact. I wouldn't be where I am today if those weren't presented to me. I know I have a long way to grow in my faith, but you have stood by my side when I was emotionally lost and when I was loving and celebrating life. You were always there.

Finally, a major shoutout to my BBTT Beta Readers! Words cannot express how grateful and thankful I am for my Beta Reader community. When I first made the announcement that I was writing a book, you all had my back and your support never waned. Thank you for all your feedback that you gave me while reading my draft manuscript. Your comments and constructive criticism all helped me to become a better writer. From the bottom of my heart, thank you all for believing in me.

Beauty Beyond the Threshold Beta Reader Community Members

Alan Turrill

Anie Baker

Ann Christie

Annie Walker

April Calvey

Ariana Perez

Ashley Stehn

Austin Mosher

Brian Werner

Carole Woodburn

Carter and Camie Green

Charlotte Michaela Ryan

Chris McCarr

Chris Scalsky

Ciera Wood

Cindy Oas

Cindy, My Mom

Connie Smith

Crystal Mitchell

Cynthia Perry

Dad

Daniel Noll

Danielle Winkler

David Williams

Dawn Doss

Daysia Guadalupe Haliburton

Deanna Amodeo

Deborah Hargreaves

Diana Nichols

Dmitriy Zakharov

Dylan Luong

Elizabeth Jenkins

Eric Koester

George Johnson

Giulia Jole Sechi

Jacob Jewell

Jacqueline Colvin

Jennifer Culp

Jennifer Kozich

Jenny Bilskie-Smith

Karen Cotter

John Moore

Kathy Besecker

Katie Baxter

Katrina Remley

Kelsey Walters

Kevin Rodriguez

Kristie Chertow

Kristina Smith

Kristy Jewell

Krystal Singley

Leah Sanson-Miles

Lee Davison

Lindsay Redwinski

Lisa Myers

Matthew Fickner

Michele Maglich

Natalie Wood

Nicholas D'Souza

Nicholas Gorza

Nicole Spindler

Olivia Sartain

Patty Kasten

Paul Farley

Paul Passfeld

Phil Meng

Phillip Sidebotham

Phillip Wilcox

Pieri Burton

Priyanka Surio

Rachael Okun

Ramonita Guadalupe

Robert "Tim" Gudge

Robert "Randy" Raley

Ron McKinnon

Samantha Savage

Scott Bland

Serena Denson

Sheila Cardoso

Sheila Vinyard

Steven Elgersma

Sue Baxter

Terry Pogue

The Maucher Family

Timothy Simmons

Tracy Neer

Uncle G.

Veronique Guadalupe

Weston Bland

APPENDIX

PROLOGUE
Goodreads. "Shannon L. Alder Quotes- Quotable Quote." Accessed June 9, 2020. https://www.goodreads.com/quotes/736100-life-always-begins-with-one-step-outside-of-your-comfort.

World Health Organization. "Depression." Accessed August 3, 2020. https://www.who.int/news-room/fact-sheets/detail/depression

CHAPTER FIVE
Penguin Random House Canada. "Excerpt from *The Journey from Abandonment to Healing: Revised and Updated.*" Accessed May 30, 2020. https://www.penguinrandomhouse.ca/books/315806/the-journey-from-abandonment-to-healing-revised-and-updated-by-susan-anderson/9780425273531/excerpt

CHAPTER TEN
National Weather Service. "Hurricane Florence: September 14, 2018." Accessed August 31, 2020. https://www.weather.gov/ilm/HurricaneFlorence

CHAPTER FIFTEEN

Encyclopaedia Brittanica Online. Academic ed. s.v. "Sanctity of the cow." Accessed April 6, 2020,
https://www.britannica.com/topic/sanctity-of-the-cow

CHAPTER SEVENTEEN

Choice Humanitarian. "Culture Preservation in Nepal." Accessed June 19, 2020.
https://www.choicehumanitarian.org/culture_preservation_nepal

Nepal Tour Guide Team, Trek & Expedition (P.) LTD. "Martyr's Day in Nepal." Accessed June 19, 2020.
https://www.tourguideinnepal.com/blog/martyrs-day-in-nepal/